To

From

Date

ONE DAY BETTER
A SPORTS DEVOTIONAL

by Jere Johnson

summerside
PRESS

One Day Better (Girls) © 2009 by Jere Johnson

ISBN 978-1-935416-15-9

All rights reserved. No part of this book may be reproduced, stored, or transmitted in any form by any means, electronic, mechanical, photocopy, recording, or otherwise, without prior permission from the publisher, except as provided by United States of America copyright law.

Special thanks to FCA's *Sharing the Victory* magazine (www.sharingthevictory.com) for use of their material and to these athletic teams for permission to reprint: North Carolina State University/Kay Yow and the University of Oklahoma/Courtney Paris. Thanks also to Derwin and Presley Gray, Stefanie Otto, Tanya Crevier, Leah Rush, and Nicole Sheaffer for their involvement with this project and the photos provided. Other photo credits: Tanya Crevier courtesy of Bruce Crevier. Kay Yow courtesy of Karl DeBlaker.

Scripture quotations marked HCSB have been taken from the Holman Christian Standard Bible © copyright 2000 by Holman Bible Publishers. Used by permission. Scripture quotations marked NLT are taken from the *Holy Bible*, New Living Translation, copyright © 1996. Used by permission of Tyndale House Publishers, Inc. Wheaton, Illinois 60189, U.S.A. All rights reserved. Scripture quotations marked NIV are taken from the Holy Bible, New International Version®. NIV®. Copyright © 1973, 1978, 1984 by International Bible Society. Used by permission of Zondervan. All rights reserved. Scripture quotations marked ESV are taken from The Holy Bible, English Standard Version®, copyright © 2001 by Crossway Bibles, a publishing ministry of Good News Publishers. Used by permission. All rights reserved. Scripture quotations marked CEV are from the Contemporary English Version, Copyright © 1991, 1992, 1995 by American Bible Society. Used by permission.

Cover and interior design by Kirk DouPonce of DogEared Design | www.DogEaredDesign.com. Typesetting by James Baker of James Baker Design | www.jamesbakerdesign.com.

Published by Summerside Press, Inc., 11024 Quebec Circle, Bloomington, Minnesota 55438 | www.summersidepress.com

Summerside Press™ is an inspirational publisher offering fresh, irresistible books to uplift the heart and delight the mind.

Printed in China.

I would like to dedicate this book to the following people:

My Lord and Savior Jesus Christ...
for without Him nothing would be possible for me.
1 Corinthians 10:31

My beautiful wife, Stacey...
who has inspired me to be a better husband, father, and friend.

My wonderful children Lauren, Caleb, and Evan...
you give me the joy of being your dad each day.

My parents, Jim and Carolyn Johnson...
who taught me to believe in myself no matter what happens in life.

My mentors, Chuck Mealy and Aidan McKenzie...
who have encouraged me to be all I can be for Christ and to serve others first.

Finally, my son, Luke Robert Johnson...
who during his short life inspired me to write, to love, to learn, and to lean
on the One who gives and takes away. Luke, I write today because of you.
Enjoy heaven until we meet again someday.

CONTENTS

FOREWORD
BY DAN BRITTON

Time usually does one of two things—bring you closer to God or draw you further away from God. One thing is for sure. You never just stay the same. Each day, you choose to move into a growing relationship with Jesus or move away from the Lord.

The book you are holding in your hands will challenge you to dig deep. *One Day Better* by Jere Johnson is a book that will help move you into a passionate relationship with Jesus. If you just want to be the same old athlete, then I encourage you to give this book to someone who wants to grow and learn. Each sports devotion will develop your spiritual foundation so that Christ will take you to a deeper level. Also, the "Get Real with God" stories will inspire you as professional athletes, top college players, and coaches share their spiritual insights.

The Lord wants to work in your life in a powerful way through this devotional book. He will shape, mold, and form you to be a true woman of God. God wants to give you boldness in your spirit to love God without limits or hesitations. Your spiritual confidence in Christ is much more important than your athletic confidence. You will be motivated to let the Holy Spirit control the very core of your life, from the inside out!

I have personally been reading Jere's devotions for years. His devotions have trained me spiritually and pushed me to love God. Being an athlete, you know a good workout produces a ton of sweat. I love to sweat because it means that I am accomplishing something. In 1 Timothy 4:7–8, Paul writes "Train yourself to be godly. For physical training is of some value, but godliness has value for all things" (NIV). The word *train* in Greek means to exercise or work out. God desires us to have "spiritual sweat"—training for godliness. "Spiritual sweat" comes when we get alone with our Savior and spend intimate, deep, rich time in the Word. He works us out—dealing with sin and revealing areas that need to be changed in our life. This only comes during our times with our Lord. *One Day Better* will produce spiritual sweat in your life.

Get plugged in and start reading *One Day Better* today. It will be your decision to move toward God. It might be one of the most important decisions you make.

Dan Britton
Sr. Vice President of Ministry Advancement
Fellowship of Christian Athletes

INTRODUCTION

As I grew up in Indiana, basketball was always part of my life. When I got a new basketball, I would play with it until it was smooth and about ready to pop. I worked hard to become a better player. I was fortunate to play three years of varsity high school basketball and learned many valuable lessons which have carried me throughout life.

The love of basketball took me into over twenty years of coaching, but in 1999, my life as a coach was turned upside down. My third child, Luke, was born with many special needs and required close to three months in the hospital before he could come home. Luke struggled with health conditions for his entire life of two years before God called him home. I learned during his life what it meant to be one day better. Every day that we went to the hospital to see him, we wanted to see progress. We wanted to see improvement. We wanted to see him getting better each day. He did get better, but in December 2001, Luke went to be with the Lord. His life is now better than ever, and he finally gets to run the streets of gold. The Lord gave me the gift of writing during Luke's life and now has given me the opportunity to start my own sports devotional site at www.sportsdevo.com.

As I continue to work with student athletes through the Fellowship of Christian Athletes or the youth sports that I coach, I strive to use the same One Day Better principle in their athletic lives. Too many athletes today do not put in the effort it takes to achieve the goals in their sport. They want the end results without all the work it takes to get there. I challenge my athletes with the question, "What are you going to do today to be better than yesterday?" They have to think and be prepared to respond immediately. The response I hear is always interesting, but it gives them a goal to strive for that day and beyond.

Having the opportunity to serve the Lord through FCA, my challenge to student athletes and coaches is to use the One Day Better principle in their spiritual walk, as well. We need to strive to grow in Christ each day through reading His Word, prayer, and fellowship with others who will encourage us in our walk with Christ.

As you read through this devotional book, I pray that it will help you draw closer to Christ. You will be inspired by the "Get Real with God" sections. Take the next thirty days to read through this book, write down your thoughts and prayers, and decide for yourself to become "One Day Better" as an athlete, friend, and one who wants to grow in Christ. May this book be a blessing to your life as you strive to live for Him!

*Expect great things from God,
attempt great things for God.*

William Carey

Game Day

READY:

"Jesus said to him, 'Away from me, Satan! For it is written: "Worship the Lord your God, and serve him only" ' " (Matthew 4:10 NIV).

SET:

Take a deep breath.... Can you smell it? The air puts a special swagger in your step.... Can you feel it? Today is not any other day—it's game day! Thoughts and feelings rush through our minds as we wait for game time to arrive. I can still feel, hear, and see the home crowd at our basketball season opener as if it was just yesterday. The songs of the band, the smell of popcorn, the sounds of people anxiously awaiting what the team would give the crowd...

Every player and coach works for one thing: game day. Game day is about mental and physical preparation for the battle ahead. Game day is here now. Let the game begin! Our Lord and Savior is no stranger to competition. I believe He was extremely competitive. Actually, He was the all-time, undefeated champion of love! He competed everyday against His archrival, the prince of darkness, the scum of the earth, the demon of the depths: Satan himself. Satan tempted, attacked, and hounded Jesus, hoping He would break. But He never did.

But Satan did not give up. He just moved on to other prey. Easy targets, weak souls, those who were ready to give up on the Lord for a piece of the second-best. Yes, people just like you and me! You see, teammates, every day is game day if you follow Jesus Christ! You have to be ready to battle the enemy every day just like Christ did. Satan knew He was no match for Jesus—but he knows he can get to us, and he knows where we are weak. When Satan tempted Jesus before He started his public ministry, Jesus put up with Satan until He had had enough and told him to get out of town. He basically said, "Be gone, Satan, because I am going to serve My God and only My God, period. You got it this time?" Satan got the message quite well, but he is still out there, daily battling with you and me and trying to defeat us.

Now, we know the game plan, because we have the playbook of God's Word. So why are we so easily defeated? Simple... We take our eyes off our goals and off our Coach and keep them on ourselves. When this happens, we are no match for the evil one. In sports, we prepare to near perfection as game day draws near. Why can't we do that for every day that we face the dark side? Why go to battle with a butter knife when you can have the sword of the Spirit on your side? Let's treat every day as game day for Christ. Just as He battled and won over sin and death, He desires for us to do the same with His help! He wants to be on your sideline today. Will you let Him? Game day is here; game day is now! The battle is upon you. Are you ready to fight?

GO:

1. How do you athletically prepare for game day?

2. Do you see every day as a spiritual game day? How can you begin to think this way?

3. What can you do to be prepared every day to battle Satan and his team?

WORKOUT:

Matthew 24:42–51
Romans 13:8–14

What Are You Looking For?

"The one who searches for what is good finds favor, but if someone looks for trouble, it will come to him" (Proverbs 11:27 HCSB).

SET:

Have you ever heard the old saying, "Whatever you're looking for, you're bound to find it"? It sure rings true today. And the trouble is that many people are searching in all the wrong places.

What about you? What are you looking for? Are you looking for the good things in life? Proverbs 11 teaches that if we look for good, then good things are bound to happen. But if we look for bad or evil things, watch out...we will probably find what we're looking for. What about when dealing with your friends and others? Do you look for the good in them, or are you looking for something bad to use against them? Just remember that what you find you will have to deal with as well.

I know a man who sees the good in everyone. He may not care for everyone, but he always looks past the bad to see the good. What a great trait to have! It's important to seek the good in everything: spiritual truth, scripture memorization, eternal memories with loved ones, and so on. But too many times we seek the immediate, quick fixes that take us down the wrong roads. One way to always find the good, however, is to keep Jesus first! When He is in control, the good rises to the surface. When we resist Him,

bad things are bound to happen.
So, today, choose Jesus and the
good that comes with Him!

GO:

1. What are you searching for? *Help!*

2. Do you find the good in life and in others? *i try, tends to be hard*

3. How can you start to look for the good and put off the bad? *Think more positively*

WORKOUT:

Psalm 34:10–14 *— look for good; negative = evil*
Psalm 122:9 *— seek good ; for God does the same*
Proverbs 11 *— Proverbs 11: 9, 17 ~ KEY VERSES*
1 Peter 3:11 *— get rid of evil, absorb all the good.*

Talk Is Cheap

"To the pure, everything is pure, but to those who are defiled and unbelieving nothing is pure; in fact, both their mind and conscience are defiled. They profess to know God, but they deny Him by their works. They are detestable, disobedient, and disqualified for any good work" (Titus 1:15–16 HCSB).

SET:

I had many favorite sayings as a coach. Here are some of them:

- Rule 1: The coach is right. Rule 2: If you think Coach is wrong, see Rule 1.
- Whether you can or can't, you are right.
- Don't tell me. Show me.

The last one may have been my favorite. Athletes have a hard time backing up what they say. They talk a good game, but many times today's athletes can't show it by their actions. All in all, talk is cheap.

In the book of Titus, Paul encouraged true believers to stand strong. Many people in that time were all talk and didn't live up to their words, especially when it came to Christ. Paul called these kinds of people despicable, disobedient, and worthless for doing anything good. Wow. Tough words, huh?

In James, we find a simple message: Do not just talk or listen to the Word, but be doers of it (James 1). Christ said that if you are going to tell Him you love Him, also show Him. Peter was a prime example of cheap talk. His heart was good, but he did not always walk his talk and did not consistently show Christ that his talk was a reflection of his true belief.

All coaches want to believe that their players will do what they say all the time, but they know that that's not always the case. If your coach can convince your team to talk less and do more, you are likely to find a greater level of success in your sport. Jesus wants the same for His believers. He wants us to talk less about all the great things we intend to do for Him and just start doing them. He wants a lifestyle of action, not one of mere talk. Athletes and Christians need to heed the same message: Talk is cheap, and action is everything.

GO:

1. Are you normally a talker or a doer? When have you been a doer? *Talker ~ on the soccer field*

2. In your life, where do you find that you are a cheap talker?

3. Today, how can you show Christ that you want to keep Him first in all you do? *Acknowledge Him and give Him the honor in all I do.*

WORKOUT:

James 1:22–25
James 2:14–26
1 John 3:18–20

The Right Path

"So follow the way of good people, and keep to the paths of the righteous" (Proverbs 2:20 HCSB).

It was the biggest race of the season. All the runners were ready to go. The rugged course was full of hills and rough terrain, but it was the race of the year. Every runner was excited to get started. With a single shot, the runners raced toward the opening in the woods. Early in the race, seven runners broke from the pack and came to a fork in the path. The lead runner made the choice, and each runner followed in stride.

In sports today, there are leaders and followers. Some leaders set a great example, but others struggle to make the right decisions, thus leading others astray. They may be leaders, but they are leading their teammates down the wrong paths. Many young athletes are very impressionable. They are looking for leadership above them and will follow those leaders on and off the floor. It takes an athlete who is strong in mind, body, and spirit to discern the right path to follow. Most can easily be led the wrong way. We need to apply today's verse and follow those who stay on the right path both on and off the field of competition.

As the seven runners blazed down the path, they quickly realized that they were running the wrong way. This mistake caused all seven to finish at the back of the pack, thus losing the big race. Today, ask yourself whom you are following. What path are they taking you down? Is yours the straight and narrow path of the righteous or the wide road to destruction? If you are on the wrong path, turn around! Head back in the other direction. It is never too late to turn around and go the right way! Once you are on the right path, continue to follow it until you reach your goal...your heavenly goal.

GO:

1. Is someone leading you astray? How?

2. Are you leading others down the wrong path?

3. What path are you currently on, and where will it eventually lead?

4. Today, how can you start and stay on the right path of life?

WORKOUT:

Proverbs 2
Matthew 5:16
Matthew 7:13–14

Commitment 101

"Commit your activities to the LORD and your plans will be achieved" (Proverbs 16:3 HCSB).

"Commitment" is a big buzz word in sports today. Coaches are asking for commitment, players want to be committed, and schools are looking for a four-year commitment. But the word "commitment" is also used very loosely these days. I personally believe we need more athletes who are committed to their academic success before their athletic careers, but I'm old-school on that one.

When it comes to commitment, Jesus Christ wants us to be committed as well. He desires our commitment. When is the last time you said, "Lord, I am committing this to You"? In the verse for today, we read that if we commit our work to the Lord, our plans will succeed. Now, that does not say we will win, but we will be successful. When we walk with the Lord, we are guaranteed ultimate victory with Him in the end.

Committing everything to the Lord is a moment-by-moment adventure, not just a one-and-done. Everything we do, everything we are, everything about us needs to be completely committed to Christ. Wow! You might say that sounds like a lot to ask, but it is the *only* way we can be totally committed to Christ. Anything less just doesn't add up. Are you struggling with commitment in life? If so, first commit all that you are to Christ and then go from there. Once you are fully committed to Him, things will work out in the end.

1. How committed are you?

2. In terms of percentage, how committed are you to Christ?

3. How can you start being committed to Christ with all that you are?

WORKOUT:

Psalm 37:4–6
1 Peter 4:19
Revelation 3:15–16

GET REAL WITH GOD

I grew up in a home where Christ was the foundation and church was a constant. My parents were exemplary models of walking the Christian walk, and Christian support surrounded me on a daily basis. So when I'm asked "When did God became real?" I have a hard time picking a single point in time, because I grew up feeling God's strong presence at various stages throughout my life.

My mom told me that when I was three or four years old, she would occasionally hear me in my room saying heartfelt prayers. Though I can't remember it, I'm sure that at that point in my life, God was as real as my neighborhood playmates. As a ten-year-old, my adventuresome nature took over, and I once rode my bike much further than I ever should have. I was lost for what seemed like an eternity, and I remember praying and asking God for direction so I could get home. I eventually found my way back and truly felt like God was guiding me home. Nothing could have convinced me otherwise. As a senior in high school, dealing with recruiting and picking a college, God again came through in a big way, making His presence known to me.

As I've grown in age, my intellect has grown, as well. I am a skeptic by nature. I ask a lot of questions and rarely am satisfied with the answers I get. As a Christian, that can be difficult. God is incomprehensible. His wonder is beyond anything I can imagine. And in a world that can make Christianity look like a crutch for the weak or a choice of the ignorant, seeing the *realness* of God can be challenging. Throughout high school and college, God seemed to come

LASTING FAITH
BY LEAH RUSH

around in very real ways here and there, though He never seemed to "stay" as long as I wished. Now I've finally learned and accepted that God will always have His hand on my life but it can look different at different times. I anticipate the times God's presence seems thick and tangible, but I have come to appreciate the times when I must truly seek.

C. S. Lewis is one of my favorite authors. And in his book *The Screwtape Letters*, Lewis writes from the perspective of a demon, explaining to his young nephew, how God operates. One section is particularly applicable and provides some insight to God's methods:

> Sooner or later He [God] withdraws, if not in fact, at least from their conscious experience, all those supports and incentives. He leaves the creature [human] to stand up on its own legs—to carry out from the will alone, duties which have lost all relish. It is during such trough periods, much more than in peak periods, that it is growing into the sort of creature He wants it to be. Hence the prayers offered in the state of dryness are those which please Him best. He wants them to learn to walk and must therefore take away His hand; and if only the will to walk is really there He is pleased even with their stumbles. Our [demons'] cause is never more in danger than when a human, no longer desiring, but still intending, to do our Enemy's [God's] will, looks around upon a universe from which every trace of Him seems to have vanished, and asks why he has been forsaken, and still obeys.

GET REAL WITH GOD

Christianity is a lot like sports. We can never reach perfection; our work is never done. Just as an athlete must continually practice to perfect their jump or swing, Christians must continually strive to keep God *real* in their lives. Yes, He will always be there. But the full value of living a life in Christ is not only *knowing* He is there but also in recognizing and responding to His presence. It is important to know that the Christian life is a struggle and requires continual work to *keep* God real. Whether we daily hear God in our lives or we have faith only as big as a mustard seed, God calls us to live a certain way, and we can oblige.

Leah Rush is a WNBA player who has been on several teams. She is currently playing in Europe, as well. Leah was a strong leader for Christ while in college at Oklahoma.

LASTING FAITH
BY LEAH RUSH

Snowflakes

"I praise you because I am fearfully and wonderfully made; your works are wonderful, I know that full well" (Psalm 139:14 NIV).

SET:

Athletes are like snowflakes. Let me explain. They come in all shapes and sizes. Many are similar in their traits and looks, but no two athletes are the same—just like snowflakes. That is what makes them so unique. Each have their qualities that, when combined with a group, can make a difference in the outcome of an event.

Do you know that God made you like a snowflake? I know, you're thinking, *Did he just call me a flake?* Well, if the shoe fits... No, seriously—God made you like no other. Even twins that look identical on the outside have something that makes them different. The psalmist writes, "I am fearfully and wonderfully made...." People sometimes have a problem with not being like someone else. We all know people we long to be like or wish for some of their abilities or traits, but we need to be content with who God made us to be. He loves us just as we are and wants us to be more like Him each day.

So as far as I can tell, it's cool to be a flake...a snowflake for Christ! Be different; be unique for Him and His glory. You have the abilities that God has given you so you'll use them for Him. Who cares if you can't dunk or hit a ball 500 feet? You have something God has given you

that He has given no one else...
that is simply being *you* and who
He created *you* to be. Use your abilities
and gifts with others to make something
special for Christ!

GO:

1. How caught up are you in trying to be someone you're not?

2. Is it difficult for you to accept who God has made you to be? Why?

3. Today, how can you be a "snowflake" for Christ, uniquely different for *Him*?

WORKOUT:

Genesis 1:27
Isaiah 43:1
Ephesians 2:10

Heart of a Competitor

"The godly walk with integrity; blessed are their children who follow them" (Proverbs 20:7 NLT).

Ready...Set...Go—and they were off! Sixty junior-high cross-country runners, heading for the first hill. They ran all over the park—a 1.5-mile course through woods, hills, and around playgrounds. Jay, a seventh-grade boy, was leading the field about halfway through the race. As they turned for the woods, Jay and the runner behind him approached a turn. Jay went on one side of the cone, his competitor the other. The race continued...but Jay turned around.

Integrity is a word that many use today but few truly understand. It is defined as moral character, honesty, and soundness throughout. David, in his psalms, emphasizes integrity and relates it to the heart. Integrity is a heart issue and affects everything we do. Integrity is doing the right thing when no one is looking. That's a big challenge for all of us to follow.

Jay had turned around because he believed he went on the wrong side of the cone. As he backtracked, his competitor distanced himself from Jay and the rest of the runners. Jay knew he needed to do the right thing. He was raised by godly parents who taught that, no matter what the cost, you always do the right thing. Jay used tremendous energy to get back up to second place after many runners passed him during his detour. He battled until the final turn and raced for the finish line. He did not win the race, as he was beaten by a teammate in the last ten yards, but he did finish third. After the race Jay would say, "I wanted to stop and cry because I knew I had made a wrong turn, but I could not give up." Jay's effort may not have won him the race, but his character and integrity showed many people the true heart of a competitor for Christ.

Jay made the right choice at the right time in the right place. Can you say the same? Coach isn't watching, but are you going hard at it?... The office will never miss that extra paper or materials, you think, as you slide them into your backpack.... Mom and Dad aren't home so I can do whatever I want on the computer.... These may all happen daily, but remember that there is always Someone watching and waiting for you to make the right choice at the right time in the right place. Christ's desire is for you to do the right thing. Show the heart of a competitor and do not give into temptation. Live to win. Your integrity is at stake.

GO:

1. When have you had to make a decision like Jay's?

2. How would someone say your integrity measures up?

3. How are you living today for God in what you do, say, and think?

WORKOUT:

James 1:22–25
James 2:14–26
1 John 3:18–20

Identity Crisis

"I am at rest in God alone; my salvation comes from Him" (Psalm 62:1 HCSB).

Athletes are trained to be a certain way. They are trained to be tough, invincible, and strong. Coaches work hard to create identities for their players—but for many of these athletes, once their playing days are over, they struggle to find who they are. They've only ever seen themselves as athletes.

The opening line of the Fellowship of Christian Athletes Competitor's Creed makes a bold statement: "I am a Christian first and last." The identity is stated clearly. I do not read where it says "I am an athlete first and last." No, it says Christian—a Christ-follower. Our identity should be found in Christ, not in our sport.

This is easier said than done, and I know from experience. When I finished coaching, I had a rough time at first. I got depressed and angry and was downright rotten to be around, but my self-pity party was interrupted one day when Christ told me I was in the wrong. When I was in His Word, He showed me over and over that sports were what I did, not who I was. Now my identity is found in Christ. He is who I am. He is who I live for. Not my sports, not my family, not my job, but for Him and Him alone. So when my job, sport, or any other part of my life goes south, I can still rejoice in the One who created me.

If you are struggling from day to day with your identity, look up and smile. The One who created you will be faithful until He calls you home to be with Him. Remember, what you do does not make you who you are!

GO:

1. When have you had an identity crisis? Are you in one now?

2. How does what you do interfere with who God has called you to be in Him?

3. What do you need to change in order to start rooting your identity in Christ?

WORKOUT:

Psalm 61:1–8
Psalm 119:17–20
Colossians 3:2

Tough Love
BY LAUREN JOHNSON

"Don't just pretend to love others. Really love them. Hate what is wrong" (Romans 12:9 NLT).

When you are playing a sport, teammates are the most important people with you. Sometimes it's hard to love them, and it can be even harder to stand up for what you believe when you are around them. The devil is always around, disguised, to make it tough. The devil even can be wearing the same jersey as you.

I learned this lesson last basketball season. I was the newbie, the one no one knew. On the day of tryouts, I only knew one other girl. I saw others in the hall, but we didn't talk. It was hard to start a new season with only a couple of friends.

It was about halfway through the season when things got shaky. One of my closest friends on the team was with another teammate who was known for gossiping...a lot. I knew this other player didn't like me—it had been pretty clear since the first week of practice—but she had never verbalized anything to me. She did talk to my friend and other teammates, though, about how annoying I was and how I shouldn't play with the "A" girls because I wasn't good enough. My friend told me that they were talking about me, and it hurt to know that my own team would do that.

Later, at practice, I was stuck guarding this other girl, and she purposely pushed me and then accidentally scratched me. It bugged me like crazy. I had always tried to love her like the Bible says we are to love others, but this was really hard for me. It was even harder to love her when I heard her talking to other girls about our teammates. She made it very difficult to be a loving Christian teammate.

When I found Romans 12:9, I thought it was pretty ironic. It was such a God thing. I knew there were numerous places in the Bible where it talks about loving your enemy, but when I found this verse I realized that I *needed* to really love her and not just act as if I did. I knew that I was just pretending to be her friend and that I actually felt hatred toward her. As the season continued, I prayed that God would help me show love to her.

As you go through your seasons and have girls on your team like the one I had, just remember what God commands us to do by loving our enemies. Pray to Him and let Him show you how to love difficult people.

GO:

1. Is there a person you need to start loving? Who is it?
2. What makes it so hard for us to love our enemies?
3. What are some ways you can show love towards teammates that are hard to love?

WORKOUT:

Romans 5:5
1 Corinthians 13:7
Matthew 5:43–44, 47

Who, Me?

"Above all else, you must live in a way that brings honor to the good news about Christ. Then, whether I visit you or not, I will hear that all of you think alike. I will know that you are working together and that you are struggling side by side to get others to believe the good news" (Philippians 1:27 CEV).

SET:

Every team needs leaders on and off the field who set the example at practice, in the classroom, and with their friends. Leaders show the way to work in all areas of their lives. Many players do not want that responsibility, but as teammates, all athletes can be leaders. Athletes are under the microscope. People are watching. Peers are watching. Fellow athletes are watching. I encourage athletes when I share with them about being a leader, and I usually get the same response—"Who, me?" They feel that nobody is watching them or cares what they do on or off the field. I beg to differ.

Paul knew this quite well. He understood that as believers in Christ we are called to lead. He challenges us in Philippians to live in such a way that brings honor to Christ daily. And not just to live it, but to show it to others for them to follow, as well. Many believers feel that they are not spiritual leaders, but that's what we are all called to be in Christ. No, you might not be called to lead a church or go to a foreign mission field, but we all have a mission field surrounding us to daily demonstrate Christlike leadership to our sphere of influence.

So the next time you say "Who, me?" to leadership as an athlete or believer, remember that others are watching closely. Don't ruin your opportunity to show leadership by living a life not pleasing to God. The best way to blow your witness is to talk one way and act another. This affects every part of your life as an athlete and a follower of Christ. Worse yet, do not be the person no one wants to follow because of double-standard living. Who, me? Yes, you! People want to follow someone who will take them higher than they have ever been before. Be a leader, live the life of truth, and let your actions be ones that people will want to follow!

GO:

1. What leadership qualities do you see in yourself? In what areas are you already leading?

2. What are some ways you have led a double life as an athlete? As a believer?

3. How can you start to lead effectively for Christ today?

WORKOUT:

Exodus 3:11–13
1 Thessalonians 4:1
Proverbs 20:22–24

Where Is Your Heart?

"For where your treasure is, there your heart will be also"
(Matthew 6:21 HCSB).

It was Christmas 1973; everything was good with the world. Northern Indiana snow, family and friends, time to open presents... I had only one wish that year: to get a basketball. And I couldn't have been happier when my wish came true with a brand-new Wilson. It quickly became my treasure. I would play nonstop—inside, outside, hot, or cold. It was just me and my ball. I honestly had no desire to do much of anything else other than to shoot and play imaginary games in which I won any and every championship. My heart was hooked on hoops.

In Matthew 6, Jesus teaches us to not store up treasures on this earth where thieves can steal and rust can decay; rather, we should store up treasures in heaven and long for the day when we enter His presence. Today, our treasures vary from person to person. For some, it is home, family, or friends; for others it is a car or other material possessions. Still others treasure things like physical appearance. One only needs to look at his or her calendar or checkbook to see their treasures. Our treasures get our time, money, and hearts.

Even though my basketball wore out, my love for the game never did. As I graduated from college and began coaching, basketball was still my treasure. I was a Christian, but my top priority was basketball. It took the birth and death of my third child for me to understand that I was storing up treasure in the wrong things and places. My son, through his life, taught me that eternity is where my heart should be.

I would love to say that I have it all figured out regarding where my heart should be, but I sometimes get off track. My time, my money, my thoughts, and my heart are not always Christ-centered. But my prayer is that we all would ponder the paths of our feet and number of our days, keeping the first things first: our faith in Christ and the perspective of Him as Lord and Savior.

I still love basketball, but I do my best to make sure it is a distant second to my pursuit of Christ. Today, take some time to evaluate your treasures. Ask yourself, "Where is my heart?"

GO:

1. What is the top priority in your life?

2. Make a list of the things you put in front of your relationship with Christ. Pray about each one and ask God to give you guidance regarding how to change your heart.

3. How can you make Jesus Christ and God's Word your treasure today?

WORKOUT:

2 Chronicles 16:9
Psalm 90:12
Proverbs 4:26

Attitude of Gratitude

"Give thanks to the LORD, for He is good. His love is eternal" (Psalm 136:1 HCSB).

SET:

Athletes of all levels seem to feel a sense of entitlement. I have sensed over the years that there is a lack of gratefulness in them. I watch as a manager serves water to an athlete, who, in response, drops his water bottle on the ground instead of handing it back to the manager standing beside him. I see little league players get instructions from coaches, umpires, and others, only to disregard them because they think they know better. What has happened to the attitude of gratitude—of having a thankful heart for the people who serve or care enough to help?

In Psalm 136, the author wants to make a very clear point. He says twenty-six times that we should be giving thanks to the Lord. The trouble is that today we treat the Lord the same way some athletes treat those who try to help them. The Lord sends someone to encourage us, and we basically ignore their kind words. The Lord blesses us with an abundance of things, and yet we complain that we have too much stuff and clutter in our lives. All we have to do is look around.... What is there *not* to be grateful for?

The next time you see someone whose attitude is less than grateful, remind them of all we should be thankful for. The only thing we are entitled to do is give daily thanks to the Lord. Without His faithfulness, we would be lost forever. It may sound like I'm being critical here, but I'm not. I've just realized that we need to be thankful for what God has done for us. Thank You, Lord!

GO:

1. Do you have an attitude of gratitude, or are you caught up in feelings of entitlement?
2. What do you need to thank the Lord for?
3. How can you realize God's faithful love in your life today?

WORKOUT:

Psalm 148
Romans 5:8–11
Ephesians 1:6–8

Her name has often been stretched across the headlines of sports pages around the nation: Courtney Paris, University of Oklahoma All-American. Of course, it's hard not to talk about an athlete who frequently added to her growing list of NCAA records, which already stood at an astonishing sixteen at the beginning of her senior year.

But unlike many egocentric players who drool at the mention of having their name in print, Paris remains unfazed. Yes, it comes with the territory, but to her it is "irrelevant." She knows that her most significant accomplishments won't ever be listed in press clippings. Rather, they are humbly imprinted on the lives of those she influences.

Growing up the youngest of eight (her twin, Ashley, is older by only two minutes), Courtney Paris never lacked for pickup game opponents. She remembers playing hoops with her sister and brothers in the driveway of their Piedmont, California, home from as early as three years old. It was there that her dreams of one day becoming a collegiate player began.

Her siblings, who now range in height from 6'3" to 6'8",

never took it easy on her. The Paris brothers made their youngest sister work for every shot, which, according to Paris, gave her a competitive edge.

Paris's father, William "Bubba" Paris, known for his three Super Bowl victories as an offensive tackle with the San Francisco 49ers, also showed off his moves in the paint during family games. His attempts, though, proved to be more humorous than helpful.

"He didn't teach me anything about basketball because he was awful at it," Paris said and chuckled.

But what Paris's dad lacked in skill on the court, he made up for in life lessons.

"He always talked to us about being born with a purpose," Paris said of her father, who is currently an evangelist and motivational speaker. "He said that God knew that [purpose] before we were even thought of. And I just have to live that up."

That philosophy is something Paris has carried with her. And she was able to apply it to her life as a Sooner.

"I feel like basketball is my small purpose on earth," said the three-time All-American. "It's something that I can do to share my faith."

Bubba Paris was full of wisdom. As a former athlete, he also was able to give advice to his daughter regarding how to compete at the highest level. His years in the NFL taught him that sacrifice was required to perform to the best of one's ability and that, in order to keep up with the "big dogs," an athlete would have to do a bit extra each day.

Paris took that lesson seriously. She knew that the time she put in would pay great dividends.

"I saw doing extra things as a sacrifice for the team," she said. "At the end of the day, it wasn't an individual sport; it was a team sport. So when I was working extra hard and my teammates were working extra hard, it was going to help all of us."

Don't be misled by her strong jaw and stern expression. Paris is gentle and soft-hearted...off the court. On the court is a different story. She didn't become the first collegiate player, male or female, to tally 700 points, 500 rebounds, and 100 blocked shots in a single season by having a powder-puff attitude on the floor.

Outside of basketball, she catches people off guard with her unassuming disposition. She is a soft-spoken young woman who loves to read, watches HGTV, and is passionate about becoming a novelist one day. She doesn't sweat the small stuff and strives to find the good in every situation. She owns a home with her sister, one they bought with money they saved by waiting tables at Sooner Legends, a barbecue restaurant in Norman. She says that "keeping a messy room" is her worst habit, and she wishes she could sing better. She'd more likely choose to relax at home with a few friends than be out in a crowd.

It's the unlikely profile of a player who broke the Big 12 career-blocks record midway through her junior year and welcomed 2009 by extending her NCAA-record double-double streak to 105. But Paris doesn't attribute much value to personal awards and broken records. They don't sum up the complete person.

"Courtney is not defined by what she did on the basketball court," Coach Sherri Coale said. "She played basketball, but that is not who she is. Courtney is humble. She doesn't even broach arrogance with all she has accomplished. She doesn't want it to be about her. She wanted it to be about her team. The double-doubles weren't important to her. If she played poorly and we won, you would never see her dejected. She has a real nice way of being about the final product, and I think that is very much a Christlike characteristic."

Whether it was sacrificing sweat and blood with a close-knit family of players in pursuit of a national championship or being a strong presence for FCA on campus, Courtney Paris counts every moment of her OU experience a blessing.

"Sometimes I think that I don't deserve the things that happen to me, like my career at Oklahoma," she said. "But God has shown me so much favor, and I am just so blessed and happy to be a part of it and work for Him."

Courtney Paris was the first player to be named First Team All-American for all four years with the Oklahoma Sooners. She holds many school and national records. Playing with her twin sister, Ashley, she worked to develop leadership skills on and off the court. In 2008, her senior year at OU, she helped to create a leadership team for her FCA huddle.

When Is Enough, Enough?

READY:

"Because of the LORD's great love we are not consumed, for his compassions never fail. They are new every morning; great is your faithfulness" (Lamentations 3:23 NIV).

SET:

Running up the score, pressing until the final whistle, up sixty points, playing starters in the fourth quarter, scoring the tenth touchdown of the game, keeping the number-one scorer in to pad her stats... When is enough, enough? We see this in everyday adult sporting events, and it is beginning to creep into the youth sports movement. Okay, let me set the record straight. I am as competitive as the next person and have had my fair share of blowouts both for and against me in my days as a player and as a coach—but at what point does compassion versus competitiveness need to be addressed?

What if Christ turned the tables and showed us no compassion? What if we asked for forgiveness and He said no? What if, when we were looking for a helping hand, He said, "Do it yourself"? Why is it that we expect God's mercy and compassion but have very little to give of our own? He shows us His compassion according to the greatness of His love for us. Maybe today we can do the same for someone else.

Now, I don't want any team to lay down and roll over just to let another team compete with

46

them, but consider everyone involved. Games will be won and lost by all teams, but they can be won with dignity and compassion. The answer to the question "When is enough, enough?" lies within you.

If or when I get back to coaching, I will be faced with this issue again. I hope I do all I can to show compassion to my opponent while battling to the end, trying my best to win the game. Compassion does not mean giving in, just acknowledging a need and doing something about it. God has done that for you. Maybe it is your turn now.

GO:

1. What does "compassion" mean to you?

2. How can you show compassion without sacrificing performance?

3. Today, how can you start showing compassion in your life and in your sport?

WORKOUT:

Matthew 5:7
Philippians 2:1–2
1 Peter 3:8

The Hot List

"Six things the LORD hates; in fact, seven are detestable to Him: arrogant eyes, a lying tongue, hands that shed innocent blood, a heart that plots wicked schemes, feet eager to run to evil, a lying witness who gives false testimony, and one who stirs up trouble among brothers" (Proverbs 6:16–19 HCSB).

There are some things that just set off a coach. Together those things make up what I call my "Hot List"—things that made me mad fast!

1. A lazy player.
2. Someone who is constantly late.
3. Those who would rather complain than try harder.
4. Those who blame everyone else and never take responsibility for their own actions.

Players like that really pushed me to the limit as a coach. Was there redeeming value in them? Absolutely. But rarely did they see it in themselves.

Many coaches have a "Hot List," and theirs may include more things than what I listed. But did you know that the Lord has a list as well? It includes arrogance, deceit, evil thoughts and actions, grumbling, and more. And what's more, the Lord says He won't put up with it. Sure, He is patient, kind, and loving, but He is also fair, just, and a God of discipline. The more you

48

know and love God, the more you will want to stay away from His "Hot List" sins.

There are many things that are out of a player's control both on and off the court, but there are also many things they can control. As a player, learn what sets your coach off and then strive to work in a way that will give God the glory and honor above all else. If you do this in all things, you will surely stay out of the doghouse, and those "Hot List" items will rarely, if ever, enter your mind. My greatest advice to you today? Keep Jesus first, and everything will find its proper place!

GO:

1. How and when have you pushed your coach to the edge with your attitudes and actions?

2. Which of the seven things that the Lord hates have you engaged in?

3. How can you start keeping Jesus first in everything?

WORKOUT:

Proverbs 6
Matthew 6:33
Mark 12:30

Right Place, Right Time

"For if you remain silent at this time, relief and deliverance for the Jews will arise from another place, but you and your father's family will perish. And who knows but that you have come to royal position for such as time as this?" (Esther 4:14 NIV).

SET:

The gym was packed with screaming fans. The tension was thick. Lacey had just come into the game, her first one as a varsity player. It was late in the fourth quarter, and her team was down by one. The ball was passed to her. She began to dribble toward the basket and—it hit her foot and bounced out of bounds. Lacey thought to herself, "I don't belong out here. Why did Coach put me in? This game is too important to mess up!"

She was in the game because she was the last guard left on the bench to play. All the others had fouled out or were already in the game. Lacey picked up a loose ball and was fouled in the process. She was going to the line for a bonus one-and-one. Eyeing the basket, she let the first shot go. *Swish!* Tie game. Three dribbles, a deep breath... She focused on the rim and heard her coach say, "Lacey, it's your time. You can do it!"

When King Xerxes began looking for another queen for his kingdom, he ordered that all the beautiful women in the land be brought to the palace. After several months in the king's household, the women would be presented individually to the king, and he would choose one. Esther, of Jewish descent, had also been brought to the palace—and Esther was the one chosen to become queen! But there was a plan to kill all the Jews in the kingdom... and Xerxes did not know that Esther was a Jew. Her cousin, Mordecai, urged her to speak to the king and plead for her people, but she was hesitant. She could be killed if she went to the king without a summons! With further encouragement from Mordecai (Esther 4:12–14), she rallied the Jews to fast and pray for her, and she leaned on the Lord for help.

In the end, Esther realized that she was in the right place at the right time for her God and His chosen people. There are three things we can learn from Esther: (1) For a period of time, you may not understand God's plan and purpose for your life; (2) When you realize God's purpose, you feel empowered; (3) Taking a risk is easier when you know that God is in control.

Feel out of place in your life? Find God and join Him there. There is always room in the right place and right time with God!

GO:

1. Are you feeling out of place at school, on the team, or at home? Why is that?

2. Do you understand God's purpose for your life?

3. Are you willing to take a risk for God today? How can you show it?

WORKOUT:

Esther 8
John 14:15

Please Wait

READY:

"I wait for the LORD; I wait, and put my hope in His word"
(Psalm 130:5 HCSB).

SET:

Ever have one of those mornings where you had to wait on
everything? I had one this week. My youngest was running
late for school. I got stuck behind too many slow cars. Every
stoplight turned red right when I got there.... Everything took
too much time that morning. And that's a problem for me
because I would rather be thirty minutes early than one minute
late. Sometimes asking me to wait is like pulling teeth with no
pain medication. It's painful!

When I finally got to my desk, I read a psalm and was
reminded that waiting can be a good thing. The psalmist wrote,
"I wait for the LORD; I wait, and put my hope in His word." *Bam!*
It hit me right upside the head. I needed to hear that message
for sure.

Why is it that we are always in such a hurry these
days? We have places to go, people to see, business
to get done, deals to make, money to spend.... Hurry,
hurry, hurry. I thank the Lord for subtly reminding
me that waiting is a key part of life.

These days, most people have a hard time
waiting. We want to win the championship, get
a better job, make the starting lineup—more,
more, more; now, now, now! But God is
holding up the stop-sign of life and
asking us to be patient: "Wait. I
have something far greater

for you than all those things."
The funny thing is that when
we finally arrive at what we were so
impatient for, we often realize it isn't what
we thought it would be anyway. We need
to focus our waiting not on the situation,
but on the Savior. Not on the pressing
matter, but on the prize of heaven. If, like
me, you struggle with waiting, be patient and
let God work. Remember, His timing is perfect.

GO:

1. How often do you struggle with waiting?

2. What are you impatient about?

3. How can you be fully devoted to waiting on the Lord?

WORKOUT:

Psalm 27:14
Psalm 33:20
Lamentations 3:26

The Only Name You Need

" 'You will conceive and give birth to a son, and you will name him Jesus' " (Luke 1:31 NLT).

Recently I saw an interview where Magic Johnson was talking with LeBron James about his success in the league. The conversation turned to former players who did so well they were known by one name or nickname—athletes like MJ, Tiger, Junior, Kobe, Sweetness, Shaq, Magic, Dr. J, and now LeBron. James said he was honored to be put in such high athletic royalty with these other men, and he hoped he would be around to see the next "one-named" guy come on the scene.

God's Word is filled with one-named guys and girls—Moses, Noah, Esther, Ruth, Joseph, Daniel, Rahab, Deborah, and others—but there is one name that stands above all other names. At this name, every knee will bow and every tongue will confess that *He* is Lord. In His name, people were healed, the possessed became whole, and lives were changed. Men and women throughout history have endangered and given up their lives for this name's sake. All things were created by Him and for Him. And it all began through a young girl chosen to bear a son and call Him the name above all names...Jesus.

All those great athletes in history who attained "one-named" status never came close to what the greatest name on earth achieved for us. It is in His name we pray. You don't hear anyone pray, "Kobe, in your name we pray…." No other name fits but the name of Jesus. So as you recognize these great athletes by their one-name monikers, let's not forget that the only name you will ever need to remember is that of *Jesus*. Honor the others, but serve the greatest Name of all!

GO:

1. Who are some other athletes or people you can think of who have been given "one-named" status?

2. When you hear the name *Jesus*, what comes to your mind and heart?

3. How can you serve the "Name above all names" better today?

WORKOUT:

Acts 15:25–27
Ephesians 5:15–20
Acts 3:1–16

The Eyes of the Lord

"For the eyes of the LORD run to and fro throughout the whole earth, to give strong support to those whose heart is blameless toward him" (2 Chronicles 16:9 ESV).

One day the team was practicing, when their coach had to leave for a minute. Once the coach was out of sight, the team started acting up and shooting half-court shots. Suddenly, out of nowhere, they heard a voice say, "I saw that." One player made the comment, "Man, Coach must have eyes everywhere." In sports, the eyes of a coach are always watching even when no one thinks they are looking.

The eyes of the Lord are always watching as well. God's Word is very clear about how God is watching us. Why does He watch over us? He loves us too much not to. But I know that many still struggle with the fact that God is watching. Some see His attentiveness as His not wanting anything good to happen to us. Others look at it as though He is playing good cop/bad cop. Still others feel as if He is always trying to catch them doing something bad. These are wrong impressions of God. The eyes of the Lord watch us because He loves us.

How does it make you feel, knowing that the eyes of the Lord are watching you? As we live for Christ, it should give us confidence that He cares about us. Throughout God's Word, we read about those who found favor in the eyes of the Lord and others who did evil. When God watches you, what does He see?

Like the coach who always seems to see everything, our God does see everything, and His eyes are looking for those who want to follow Him.

GO:

1. How does it make you feel to know that God is watching over you?

2. God sees the good, the bad, and the ugly in our lives. When do you wish He was not watching?

3. What is the positive side of His seeing us during our sinful behavior?

WORKOUT:

Genesis 6:8
Psalm 34:15
Proverbs 5:21; 15:3
1 Peter 3:12

Spiritual Twinkies

"Do not love this world nor the things it offers you, for when you love the world, you do not have the love of the Father in you. For the world offers only a craving for physical pleasure, a craving for everything we see, and pride in our achievements and possessions. These are not from the Father, but are from this world. And this world is fading away...." (1 John 2:15–17 NLT).

Athletes today need the best foods to nourish their bodies for maximum performance, but every once in a while we all eat things that are not good for us. One of those snack foods that trip up many a person is the dreaded Twinkie. Did you know that over 500 million Twinkies are sold each year? That's a lot of consumed junk food. I've actually have never eaten a Twinkie, but many an Oreo has crossed my path. Now, occasional junk food is not entirely bad for us, but many times one such temptation is not enough; we continue to go back for more until we can't stop. Most people have the self-control to stop, but some cannot, and they develop a problem.

When the disciple John wrote the letter of 1 John, he talked about those who cannot stop loving the world. The world today is like a big Twinkie. Sure, it looks good...might even taste good...but it has no spiritual nutritional value for you. In my Monday morning small group, one of the men labeled the things of this world as "spiritual Twinkies"—things like most TV shows, movies, music, internet, alcohol, and on and on. Anything this world offers that has no spiritual nourishment or redeeming value, in my mind, would be considered a spiritual Twinkie.

In our verses today we see that everything on this earth is fading away. However, those who want to live their lives doing God's will can live forever with Him (see the end of verse 17). The so-called "spiritual Twinkies" can rob us from truly living for Christ. Too much of this world will only lead someone away from their ultimate goal of heaven, just as too much junk food can hinder the path of a finely tuned athlete.

I am not telling you to go throw away all your junk food, but God's Word does command us to rid ourselves of anything that keeps us from being fully devoted to Him. So, essentially, get rid of those spiritual Twinkies that are weighing you down!

GO:

1. What are you indulging in today?

2. What spiritual Twinkies are weighing you down?

3. This week, how can you be in the world but not of it?

WORKOUT:

Hebrews 12:1–2
1 Corinthians 10:13
Galatians 5:19–25

For more than thirty years, women's basketball coaches have stood on the shoulders of Kay Yow. An undeniable legend in the sport, her biography reads like an excerpt from "College Basketball's Most Desirable Accomplishments." But Yow's fiercest competitor hasn't been on the court.

The North Carolina State head coach was diagnosed with breast cancer three times—the last with Stage IV in November 2006. But as likened to any other rival, she showed up for cancer's game determined to fight. The following is a portion of an interview that FCA's "Sharing the Victory" had with Coach Yow and published in March 2008.

You've been through a lot the past two years with a cancer relapse and extensive chemotherapy. What has God taught you through this battle?

Kay Yow: He is definitely working on my character to a deeper degree. There is no question about that. You have a chance to become a stronger person—a more Christlike person—while you're going through it. And on top of that, you turn around and are being blessed in so many ways.

During road games, there are still people who applaud when I come onto the court. There are still people who come to get my autograph, to get pictures, and I sometimes feel like I need to be focused on what I am doing. But recently a gentleman came down right in front of the bench on the floor and wanted to have a picture taken, so we did. He thanked me for doing it, just for taking the time. And I thought that if it meant that much to him, I'm glad I did it.

Have you ever wondered why cancer happened to you?
KY: I've never questioned why I have cancer. I have an idea, but I know that God has a plan for me, and I just try to trust His plan and what it is that He wants me to do. That is the main thing.

I do know that He loves me and that it is a love that is deep. I know He wants the best for me. I feel sort of fortunate to even get a little bit of an answer. I wouldn't expect one, but I don't want to miss what He wants me to get out of all this.

What do you think that is? What do you think He wants you to get out of this?
KY: I think it's a lot about developing character and becoming more Christlike through it all. I know that it is about Him giving me much encouragement through His Word, and I know that He would have me give encouragement to others, which I try to do often.

I wrote a letter to a guy who was diagnosed with cancer in July [and] who just passed away in December. His people wanted me to write to him because they wanted him to be saved. I wrote to him and sent him a booklet on [the] four spiritual laws, and I was told that at his viewing, my letter was there in a frame. So I have had many opportunities to help people as a result of this battle.

Are you ever scared?
KY: I think the first year you have cancer, it is a shock. But the main thing is, if I let myself focus on the negative aspect of it, the fear would be there. To me, my whole thing is to never let my mind focus that way. If something negative enters my mind, I push it out. I focus on God because then God becomes big and the problem becomes small. But if I focus on the problem, the problem becomes big and God becomes small. So I know what I need to focus on anytime I start to doubt.

I have to tell you this. When I was first diagnosed with cancer, even the second time and at the beginning of the third time, I wanted to know everything about it. I wanted them to send me anything—everything on the Internet, articles—anything, just send it to me. But one day, I heard a statistic of people who had metastatic cancer, that the average length of time they live after being diagnosed is three years. At that point, I didn't want to know anything else.

Now I don't read anything about it. Most of all I just focus on the Lord, my job here, and my treatments. Because if [three years] is an average, then somebody had to be way up there and someone way over there to get it to that average.

What do you do to keep your joy?

KY: I talk with other people, and I encourage them to be positive. I try to share my faith with them. And if you have faith in God, He is so powerful and so strong. He can give you strength; He can give you peace; He can give you joy. And that's where it's coming from for me. You can try to get it from other places, and you can get it to a certain extent, but it's nothing like what you can get from Him.

How do you live out your faith in front of your players?

KY: Well, I think it has to be with the words I use, my actions, my responses to things that happen. I have to really be concerned about being even-keeled. I am working on not getting too high with the highs and too low with the lows—being consistent for the players. And just to treat them the way I would want to be treated.

I also try to see them for who they can become, not just for who they are now. You have to have that vision and believe in them so that you can help them believe in themselves. Many people have done above and beyond because somebody else believed in them.

Coach Yow died in January 2009 from this third round of cancer. It may have taken her life, but her legacy of faith, friendship, and fight continues to live on in the hearts of all her North Carolina State players and other players across the country. Coach Yow embodied the heart of a champion, and her passion to be "One Day Better" will never be forgotten.

It's a Choice

READY:

"But Joseph said to them, 'Don't be afraid. Am I in the place of God? You intended to harm me, but God intended it for good to accomplish what is now being done, the saving of many lives. So then, don't be afraid. I will provide for you and your children.' And he reassured them and spoke kindly to them" (Genesis 50:19–21 NIV).

SET:

Alexis was a talented basketball player. As an eighth grader, she played on the varsity team at her school. Others quickly saw her ability and soon began mistreating her. Teammates beat her down mentally, and she began to grow a root of bitterness deep inside of her. She suffered several injuries and even transferred schools, but her situation did not improve. The root grew deeper and deeper.

Joseph was a part of a team as well—a team of brothers in Jacob's household. Joseph was blessed in many ways, and his brothers soon became bitterly jealous. When he was seventeen, his brothers sold him into slavery. But Joseph kept his faith. He was later falsely accused of a crime and imprisoned for years, but thirteen years later, when he was thirty years old, he was named the second in charge of all of Egypt. Thirteen years... The root of bitterness could have grown deep in that amount of time, but Joseph, through God's help, focused on His plan for his life. When Joseph's father died, his brothers immediately worried that their brother would pay them back for all their wrongdoing. But Joseph made a choice to forgive, and he reassured his brothers of his love and faithfulness to them.

Alexis was faced with a choice, too. She could continue to be bitter, or she could forgive those in her past who had put her down and were unloving to her. In a similar way, each of us have that choice every day. We can choose to forgive and forget or choose to be bitter and hurt others in return. You may not think that your bitterness is bothering others, but trust me, it will in time. Forgiveness is *not* a two-way street. God wants you to forgive and move forward. My prayer for Alexis, myself, and others is that we make the choice, like Joseph, to forgive—every day. Because even though others may intend to hurt and harm, God can and will use bad experiences for our good.

GO:

1. How are you encouraged by Joseph's story?

2. Do you have a root of bitterness growing inside of you? How long has it been growing?

3. Today, sever the root of bitterness and seek forgiveness for this person or people in your life. Pray and ask God to help you finally forgive them.

WORKOUT:

Genesis 37–50
Hebrews 12:14–16

Awesome

"For the LORD Most High is awesome. He is the great King of all the earth" (Psalm 47:2 NLT).

The word *awesome* is used to describe so much in sports today. "Did you see that awesome catch?" "She's an awesome player!" "That home run was awesome!" I looked up this word in the Urban Dictionary. It defines *awesome* as "totally cool." It is what is called a "sticking plaster" word, which is something used by Americans to cover the huge gaps in our vocabulary. It is supposedly one of three words that make up most American sentences. And in sports today, that is definitely the case. Everything great is "awesome."

I'm afraid that we are misusing this word, however. It may be that this special word should really be reserved for God alone. It should be set apart for the One who is like no other and who will never be repeated. Let's take a look in God's Word to see what *awesome* really means. Isaiah 40:12 describes the awesomeness of God with these questions: "Who else has held the oceans in his hand? Who has measured off the heavens with his fingers? Who else knows the weight of the earth or has weighed the mountains and hills on a scale?" (NLT). Also, the first sentence in the Bible speaks of God's awesomeness: "In the beginning God created the heavens and the earth" (NLT). What more do you need? There are amazing catches, great plays, and fantastic finishes to games, but all of them have been repeated in some way, shape, or form. Only God has been unrepeated. There is no one like our God (see 1 Samuel 2:2). So when you are watching something (sports, movies, TV, whatever), call it what it is, but don't call it *awesome* unless it is about God. Work on reserving that word for the only One worthy of its acclaim. There are some things that should only ever be for Him. The word *awesome* should be on that list. Why? Because He is an awesome God!

GO:

1. How do you tend to use the word *awesome*?

2. How is God awesome in your life?

3. How can you reflect on God's awesome power today and apply it to your daily pursuits?

WORKOUT:

1 Chronicles 17:20
Psalm 99:3
Isaiah 40

The Chosen

"Therefore, God's chosen ones, holy and loved..."
(Colossians 3:12 HCSB).

Danny was not a good athlete. In fact, he was pretty bad. I
remember how he always hated recess. When we were in the
third grade, we played a killer game of kickball every recess,
and every boy played...except for Danny. He always watched
closely, though. One day the sides were uneven, and I was named
captain. I knew what I had to do. With my first pick in the 1970
First Round Draft for recess kickball, I chose Danny Anderson.
After everyone got up off the ground from laughing, Danny
walked over to my side with his head down.

We are lucky people, don't you think? What? You don't feel
lucky? You should. You have been chosen. When God looked over
all the people, He chose *you*! Isn't that awesome? Why did He
choose you? You are a sinner, the scum of the earth, a jerk by all
standards, at times. But because of His love for you and
the holiness He desires for your life—and because He
knows what you are capable of doing—He chose you
to be on His team forever!

In Matthew 4, we read that Jesus encouraged
His disciples to "come follow Me!" He chose them,
just like He chose you and me. What a great
feeling to know that not only have you been
chosen but that you are loved, as well. It
doesn't get any better than that.

Danny came over to
me and said, "Jere, what

are you thinking? I'm the worst player in class." My response was simple, "You might not be as good as some of the others, but you are the best encourager I know." With that, Danny's whole expression changed. He was right. He was a bad player and made an out every time, but you never saw anyone encourage his team to victory as much as Danny did that day. For a day, Danny Anderson was chosen. With Christ, you can be chosen, as well. Have you chosen Him to be the Lord of your entire life? He chose you. Will you chose Him?

GO:

1. Have you ever been picked first? How did it feel?

2. Have you chosen to follow Christ forever?

3. Today, what can you do to start living a life as one who has been chosen by God?

WORKOUT:

Romans 8:31–39
1 Thessalonians 1:4–5
1 Peter 2:9

In Pursuit Of...

"But just as he who called you is holy, so be holy in all you do; for it is written: 'Be holy, because I am holy' " (1 Peter 1:15–16 NIV).

Grades, money, sports, championships...the list goes on and on. These are the things we are in constant pursuit of these days. On the surface these things are not inherently bad, but are we consumed by these pursuits? I see nothing wrong with wanting good grades or to excel in sports or to ultimately win a championship during a season, but those should not be our end-all pursuits.

I have been reading an old book I got from my brother Jim for my high school graduation. I read it then, but it had very little impact on my life until I picked it up some twenty-four years later. Jerry Bridges's book, *The Pursuit of Holiness,* has rekindled the light that had gone dim over these past years. One of my favorite quotes from the book is, "God does not require a perfect, sinless life to have fellowship with Him, but He does require that we be serious about holiness, that we grieve over sin in our lives instead of justifying it, and that we earnestly pursue holiness as a way of life." Like the old Batman shows, I got a *bam, smack, pow,* right upside my head to wake me up as to what I need to be pursuing in my life.

As an athlete, what are you pursuing outside of your sporting life? Too many times we become defeated by sin and then justify it because of some life crisis we might be going through, but that just doesn't cut it by His standard. Our problem in life is that we are living by the world's standards, not God's. God's standard is pretty simple: " 'Be holy, because I am holy' " (1 Peter 1:16 NIV). We are to pursue holiness in our lives. Okay, so it doesn't sound as glamorous as pursuing a third championship win or gaining the top scholarship, but those things won't get you any closer to God. You can pursue anything in life, but the only pursuit that will make an eternal difference is your pursuit of holiness. Remember, God has called every Christian to a holy life; there is no getting around it, no matter how hard you try.

GO:

1. What are some evidences of holiness in your life today?

2. Which sins bother you enough to change and seek the help God wants to give for you to become like Him?

3. What are some specific areas of your life that will change as you begin to pursue holiness?

WORKOUT:

Genesis 2:3
Matthew 7:21–23
Exodus 15:11
1 Thessalonians 4:4

Damaging Words

"Likewise the tongue is a small part of the body, but it makes great boasts. Consider what a great forest is set on fire by a small spark" (James 3:5 NIV).

Have you ever turned a television channel to a ball game, watched as the camera zeroed in on the bench during a tough moment, and witnessed a coach or player saying words he shouldn't have said? Foul language is commonplace in athletics today. What makes the use of these words so attractive? Some say it motivates; others say it is necessary to get the point or lesson across. If that is the case, how do teachers and preachers give lessons of life without using these words? If this type of language is used to motivate, then why is over 90 percent of it used in a negative context?

In the New Testament, James shares that the tongue is a very dangerous weapon. Controlling our speech is vitally important in our spiritual journey. Often we are judged not by what we do, but by what comes out of our mouths. I've heard it said, "Swearing is the expression of a weak mind trying to express itself forcibly," and I think that's the best definition of swearing yet. I have not met an athlete or coach who would admit to having a weak mind, but such language might speak for itself. Great coaches now and in the past have had great success without using harsh language. Coach John Wooden is a good example of this. What can we learn from him? I am sure that controlling the tongue meant controlling other areas in their coaching (i.e. anger and attitude), as well.

Many athletes have said that swearing is a difficult habit to break, but guarding your tongue is a discipline that needs to be practiced just like the skills in your sport. Athletes, does swearing make you a better player? Have you considered the damage your words can do to your teammates and others around you? If not, stop right now and consider what would happen if you stopped swearing today and used different words to convey your message. Clean up the talk and see what happens. If you don't use foul language, good for you. Let your teammates know it bothers you, as well. Be the first on your team to take a stand in this important area. I guarantee you will see the difference.

GO:

1. When do you find yourself struggling with foul language?

2. When your language goes south, what goes along for the ride? Your anger, as well?

3. Today, how can you start to tame the tongue and use words that will not offend others?

WORKOUT:

James 3:1–12
Matthew 5:37

Get in the Race

"I have hidden your word in my heart that I might not sin against you" (Psalm 119:11 NIV).

It was the first race of his freshman year in high school in his small Indiana town. Was he ready? Had he trained properly? Who was the competition? These thoughts rushed through his head as he entered the starting blocks of the 400-meter relay.

Timing, precision, and teamwork were all a part of this outstanding race. Was he worthy to be on this team as a freshman and then have the extra responsibility to lead off? He had had a great junior high career, setting eight school records, but this was high school, the big time!

Feet set in the blocks...inside lane...judges ready... Teammates anxiously awaited their turn to run. Runners to your mark...set... *bang!* The young freshman dashed ahead, blazing down the track. He could hear everyone yelling his name. He was thinking he must be doing well. He looked up and saw his teammate jumping up and down with excitement as he approached the crucial point in the race, the first handoff.

Just then, he realized...all the screams and excitement were not because he had arrived first at the handoff point but because he left his baton in the starting blocks. He was so excited about his first race in high school that he'd left without the proper equipment, the one thing he needed to be a part of this important race.

Embarrassed and empty

inside, he walked off the track. Yes, he finished his day of events, but he never again forgot to start off the race right. He never again left his baton at the start. If we don't do what Psalm 119 says, we'll be like this freshman. We need God's Word each day to start off our daily race in the right way. But it does not end there. We need to daily hand off our baton (God's Word) to others, too. We need to share the goodness and grace of our loving Savior to each person we meet.

In the end, the young freshman grew up to have a great high school track career and set several records along the way—but one thing I never forgot was to carry my baton with me. Yes, that was my story. But now each day as I serve FCA in the Chicagoland area, I am challenged to start my race in God's Word so I can be ready to pass it to those around me, that they in turn can continue our race—God's race to His kingdom! God bless you as you pass on your spiritual baton to those in need!

GO:

1. When and why have you felt unprepared in a situation?
2. How often do you leave home without the right equipment and preparation?
3. How often do you start your day by spending time with God and hiding His Word in your heart?

WORKOUT:

1 Timothy 4:8
1 Timothy 4:12–16
1 Peter 3:15

Can't You Be Happy?

"But he replied to his father, 'Look, I have been slaving many years for you, and I have never disobeyed your orders, yet you never gave me a young goat so I could celebrate with my friends' " (Luke 15:29 HCSB).

Kim was a good player. She worked very hard, as hard as anyone on the team, but game after game she sat at the end of bench. Every day she did exactly what the coach said, but she rarely got to play in the games. Ashley, on the other hand, always ended up in trouble. She spent as much time in the principal's office as she did in class—and Ashley started every game. This did not go over well with Kim and her other teammates.

Luke 15 tells the story of two sons. One was obedient, hardworking, and always honored his father. The other was impetuous and never knew what he was going to do next. The younger, free-spirited son left home with his inheritance while the older son worked for his father. One day, the older son came in from the fields and saw a celebration preparation taking place. When he found out it was for his brother, he lost it. He approached his father and asked why they were celebrating his brother. He had done nothing but trash their father's name and fame. The father said he loved them equally but that the younger brother was finally home.

Back to Kim. Finally she'd had enough. She went to her coach with a resentful spirit. She accused him of showing favoritism and stated that she worked harder than this other player. The coach simply replied, "Kim, you mean as much to this team as Ashley does." Later, another girl in the same situation as Kim stopped her and asked, "Kim, why can't you just be happy for the team and keep working hard?"

We all get frustrated with our status in life. Others get the credit when we do the work, some get a break when we don't, and many get ahead when we are getting behind. It is easy to have a resentful spirit, but Christ in His abundant love reaches down and shows us how much He loves us and wants us to be more like Him. Resentment will always block our path to righteousness. When others around you succeed, be happy for them. Show them a Christlike spirit. Happiness is a choice. Whatever your lot is today, rejoice in the fact that God is giving you this opportunity to give Him glory.

GO:

1. Are you caught in a trap of resentment?
2. How can you learn from the older brother's attitude?
3. Today, how can you be happy with who you are and where God has you?

WORKOUT:

Romans 12:15
Psalm 119:1
Proverbs 8:32

GET REAL WITH GOD

God became real to me when I had nothing left. Unfortunately, this is an all-too-common scenario, but God knew best.

Much like the return of the prodigal son, I showed up on my parents' doorstep with nothing but my car and my belongings. I had narrowly escaped a life I had tried to create on my own, safe from surprises and any kind of emotion but ironically packed full of baggage, hurt, and failure.

Angered at God for what I felt was unjust treatment after trying so hard to turn my life around and live a "Christian lifestyle," I literally showed up at church with my arms crossed and a very bad attitude towards Christ and anything He supposedly stood for.

A week later, I went for a run and shouted at God, demanding an explanation. I bent down to tie my shoe and felt God say, "Sit down!" I did, and I listened. It was then that I understood why everything had happened the way it did. I had made my own mistakes; God didn't purposely plan them. I had screwed up; God had not cursed me. And finally, God wanted me to use these mistakes for His glory. I truly had nothing left, and God whispered to me, "My grace is sufficient for you. Through your weakness, my strength is made known." I cried and asked for forgiveness. I had been so selfish and had cared more about what I and others thought than truly and simply living out my life for Christ.

I have faced many trials and experienced many blessings since that morning run two years ago. But I have learned that

PRODIGAL CHILD
BY NICOLE SHEAFFER

God is faithful and can use anyone and any mistake, no matter the size, to further His kingdom. I grasp for God, breathe Him in, and lean on Him daily. Without Him, I am truly nothing.

Nicole Sheaffer was a standout high school athlete and is now working on her graduate studies in Minnesota. She still competes on a hockey and rugby team. Nicole is passionate about sharing her faith with her teammates and others.

Lost

" 'What man among you, who has 100 sheep and loses one of them, does not leave the 99 in the open field and go after the lost one until he finds it?' " (Luke 15:4 HCSB).

SET:

Can you guess what 98 percent of all athletes on team rosters have in common? What does the remaining 2 percent have that the others do not? Is it playing ability? Payroll size? Nope. It is simply a matter of location and destination.

In Luke 15, Christ tells three stories of lost items. One, a sheep; another, a coin; and the remaining, a son. All were lost, but none of them realized their situation. The sheep did not realize it was lost until the shepherd found it. The coin was content with where it was until the lady who had lost it found it. Finally, the son knew he was gone, but he did not realize he was lost until he returned home to his father.

So just what is it that separates these team rosters across the country? Only 2 percent of these athletes claim to be "Christian athletes." The rest—the other 98 percent—don't realize they are lost. They may be at the top of their game, drive the nicest cars, or make the most money, but a life without Jesus Christ is a life that is lost. No amount of success can earn eternity. Only by returning to the Good Shepherd or coming back home to the heavenly Father will one realize that they are truly found in Him, Jesus Christ. If you are one of the 2 percent of athletes who know the Light, shine on those who are lost and in the dark. Do not allow them to be lost forever. You have the map, you have the game plan, and you possess the directions to the Savior. Share the information with those in need. They may be lost for now, but don't let them be lost forever.

GO:

1. Who first told you about Christ? When did you start following Him?

2. Do you know someone who is lost? How can you recognize when someone is looking for the way?

3. How can you show the lost the way to Christ today?

WORKOUT:

Luke 15
John 14:6
Jeremiah 29:11–14

The Voice of Truth

READY:

"Teach me Your way, LORD, and I will live by Your truth"
(Psalm 86:11 HCSB).

SET:

I love sports movies, and my all-time favorite is "Hoosiers." That might have something to do with my being a former Indiana high school basketball player, and the movie was filmed in the 80s when I was in college. One scene from the movie stood out to me. During one game, Hickory (the high school) was in need of a sub, and the coach didn't have anyone to put in the game except Ollie, the manager. So Coach put him in late, and Ollie got fouled and had to go to the line for two free throws. The crowd was yelling, the opposing team was taunting, and Ollie's knees were shaking as he stepped to the line.

Throughout the Bible's history, men and women heard voices of opposition but chose to listen to the Voice of Truth. What if Moses had listened to Pharaoh or all the grumblings of the Israelites as they traveled? What if Joshua had listened to those who said they only needed to go around Jericho six times? What if David had listened to everyone who said he was too little, too young, and too weak to defeat Goliath? And what if Esther had not been brave enough to go to the king, her husband, and beg on behalf of her people? The outcome of each would have been different. These people, however, and many more throughout history, listened to the Voice of Truth—the voice of God pouring truth into their lives.

This Voice of Truth is still alive and well today.

Back to our story... Ollie stepped up to the line. In the middle of the cries of opposition, he nailed the first free throw. The other team called a time-out to "ice" him. But during the time-out, the coach said something important—that "after Ollie hits the free throw," they would run a certain defense. The coach was a confident voice of truth at that moment. Ollie stepped up and nailed the next free throw, and Hickory won the game to advance.

The popular singing group Casting Crowns sings of this Voice of Truth in a song by that title. One phrase in the song says it all: "Out of all the voices calling out to me, I will choose to listen and believe the Voice of Truth." We all have voices of opposition in our lives. Satan wants to see us fail, and he'll use many different strategies to keep us from growing in our faith. However, there is one voice that rings louder and truer than any voice I know: God's voice, found especially in His Word and in prayer.

GO:

1. Which voice do you hear in your life today? Are you listening to the right voice?

2. What does the Voice of Truth sound like to you? What do the voices of opposition sound like?

3. How much time do you spend in the Word or in prayer to be able to hear the Voice of Truth?

WORKOUT:

Psalm 29:3–4
Psalm 66:18–20

Honor Him

"Therefore, fear the LORD and worship Him in sincerity and truth. Get rid of the gods your ancestors worshiped beyond the Euphrates River and in Egypt, and worship the LORD" (Joshua 24:14 HCSB).

The sports world loves to pay tribute to great athletes and coaches. Halls of Fame, retired jerseys and retired numbers, street names and building names—all to honor famous sports heroes. But what are they really honoring? Some were great men and women off the field, but for the most part those things honor great achievements in athletics. In my book there's nothing wrong with that, until we look at whether we truly honor Christ in our sporting endeavors.

As athletes, how do we honor the Lord? Do we honor Him with our words? With our daily practice ethics? With our personal integrity? Honoring Christ is just as much an on-field endeavor as an off-field one. Are you an athlete or a Christian? Which one are you truly trying to be? Believe it or not, you *can* be both at the same time.

Joshua understood this quite well. He was a fierce leader and competitor, but he told people where he truly stood. Joshua knew that his life was supposed to honor the Lord and that he should serve Him with everything he had. He knew he needed to be both a leader and a Christian at the same time in order to give his life meaning and purpose.

Where does that leave you? Do you battle to combine your faith and your sport? If so, why? Christ doesn't want you to leave your sport, but He does want you to compete fiercely for Him and for His honor and glory. So I ask you this: Are you trying to honor Christ or yourself in your sport? If we honor Christ as we play, we will act differently, talk differently, and live differently, but that doesn't mean we have to play with less intensity.

Today, be like Joshua! Honor Christ and serve Him with all you are. Play for Him! Honor Him with all that you have! You can do it!

GO:

1. How do you honor Christ in your sport?

2. Do you honor Christ off the field?

3. How can you bring more glory and honor to Christ today?

WORKOUT:

Psalm 86:12
Mark 12:30
1 Peter 2:11–12

Do You Need Help?

"When Jesus saw him lying there and learned that he had been in this condition for a long time, he asked him, 'Do you want to get well?' 'Sir,' the invalid replied, 'I have no one to help me into the pool when the water is stirred. While I am trying to get in, someone else goes down ahead of me.' Then Jesus said to him, 'Get up! Pick up your mat and walk.' At once the man was cured; he picked up his mat and walked" (John 5:6–9 NIV).

The player was struggling, missing foul shot after foul shot in practice. Obviously frustrated, the player continued working on her game after practice. Her coach sat nearby, watching. He got up to watch more closely. Rebounding miss after miss he offered, "Do you want me to help you?" "No, I do not. I can fix my own problem," she shot back. He smiled and continued to rebound.

Our biblical example sat there by the pool at Bethesda, an invalid, for thirty-eight years. Broken in body and spirit, he sat waiting...waiting for someone to help. Jesus came by the pool one day and asked him a simple question: "Do you want to be well?" The invalid humbly spoke and said there was no one to help him into the pool to be healed. Jesus offered His help. He said, "Get up! Pick up your mat and walk!" The invalid did just that. He took Jesus at His word and followed His direction. Jesus spoke, and it happened. Another miracle, yes, but a better case made for basic belief.

After rebounding for what seemed like an eternity between makes, the girl's coach offered again. "Do you want me to help you?" Broken and in tears, she nodded. The coach made a minor adjustment to her form and said, "Try again." She eyed the basket, let the ball go, and...swish! Repeatedly she shot, making basket after basket. What made the difference? She allowed her coach to help.

Like this player, the invalid in the book of John knew he needed help. He truly desired help and healing. Jesus, the Master Coach, knows what ails you. You may not be a thirty-eight-year invalid, but you are still sick. While you are mired in sin and living a life unworthy of Christ, He offers you help. He offers His hand. He offers His healing. Will you take it or reject it? Rejecting Him once is childish, but rejecting Him repeatedly is foolish. Take Him at His word!

GO:

1. In what ways do you need help or healing?

2. When have you been too stubborn to ask for help?

3. Today, how can you start to take Jesus at His word?

WORKOUT:

Psalm 30
Matthew 11:28–30
1 Peter 2:22–25

Attacks from Within

"I became extremely angry when I heard their outcry and these complaints. After seriously considering the matter, I accused the nobles and officials, saying to them, 'Each of you is charging his countrymen interest.' So I called a large assembly against them" (Nehemiah 5:6–7 HCSB).

SET:

What's worse...being beaten by your opponent because they're better than you, or being beaten by your opponent because of internal strife within your own team? In my experience, the worst teams I've been a part of, either as an athlete or coach, were the ones with the most internal problems. Preparing for your opponent is tough enough, but trying to "right the ship" from within is a totally different animal.

As Nehemiah and his crew worked to rebuild the wall in the Old Testament, they were oppressed by outside forces. They struggled financially and started to fight, which created dissention in the ranks. It was so bad that they sold their own children into slavery. Finally Nehemiah had had enough. He put his foot down and held an "all-team" meeting. I'm sure he did most of the talking.

We all deal with internal strife within our teams, churches, families, friends— pretty much anywhere we have a group of people. Satan loves to get his foot into these areas and destroy as much as he can. Players get jealous of playing time and attention from the coaches; church members get mad because they feel snubbed by the pastor or unheard; friends overreact when they feel neglected and hurt…. Internal problems will always be a part of life, but they take our focus off the real goal and purpose. Nehemiah put the focus back on God and on uniting the body, and that is a good lesson for all of us to follow.

As Christians, we need to work toward unity, not division. If we say we walk with Christ, shouldn't we act like it? He handled it with grace and goodness, with kindness and compassion, and with life lessons and love. He faced internal issues with His disciples, but He always took their eyes off themselves and pointed them to the truth of the gospel.

So today, when attacks come from within, be part of the solution from the Savior. Do not become part of the problem from the prince of darkness.

GO:

1. What are the internal problems that are holding your team back?

2. What role do you need to play when these attacks arise?

3. Today, how can you be part of the solution instead of part of the problem?

WORKOUT:

2 Chronicles 30:12
Psalm 133:1
1 Peter 5:8

Slump

READY:

"They wander about for food and howl if not satisfied. But I will sing of your strength, in the morning I will sing of your love; for you are my fortress, my refuge in times of trouble" (Psalm 59:15–16 NIV).

SET:

Tiger Woods went a month without winning a tournament. Barry Bonds didn't homer for a week. Jeff Gordon didn't win a race for a month. These are all true career stories of the great athletes named. Sportswriters love reporting stories like these because they get to go for the jugular. They break out the big "S" word—*slump*. Sports fans and writers get used to sports heroes performing day in and day out. When the reality hits that these athletes aren't perfect, people feel as if they have to make an excuse or that something must be terribly wrong with the athlete in question. For the three examples above, I'm not sure that the word "slump" is right, but we all go through tough times in life and in sport.

Webster defines *slump* as a "slide," a "decline," or a "falling off." I can relate to the word *slump*. Recently it appeared that I was in one. I was allowing life to get the best of me. Everything in life was starting to slide...work, home, and church. I didn't want to write or even do much of anything. I was in a spiritual slump, too. Why? I'm not really sure, but I didn't have to hit a three-hundred-yard drive, a game-winning homer, or race five hundred miles at 200 mph to get out

90

of my slump. I simply turned my head toward heaven and asked for help. I had lost my joy, my happiness, my way home. I had taken my eyes off Him and concentrated on myself—but God reminded me just how good I really had it with Him and in Him. After reading the passage in Psalm 59, He showed me, as He *always* does, that His love is more than enough to sustain me and keep me happy in Him.

Are you in a slump in sport, in life, or in spirit? If so, take courage and take hold of His truth for you today. He is our refuge in times of distress, and we can shout for joy every day because of His unfailing love. Slump? What slump? God is the ultimate slump-breaker. Allow Him to help today. He works if you give Him a chance!

GO:

1. Ever feel like you are in a slump, athletically or spiritually?

2. Are you currently on a spiritual upswing or downslide?

3. How can you start to find joy in Jesus and break out of the funk?

WORKOUT:

Matthew 6:33
Romans 15:13
Hebrews 12:1–3

R U "FAT"?

"All Scripture is inspired by God and is profitable for teaching, for rebuking, for correcting, for training in righteousness, so that the man of God may be complete, equipped for every good work" (2 Timothy 3:16–17 HCSB).

I was approached the other day and asked if I was fat. Well, as a former athlete and coach who has put on a few since his glory days, I was taken aback. "I may be fat, but you're ugly," I kidded him. He laughed and responded, "Not that kind of fat!" I was interested to see how he was going to get out of this one.

He went on to tell me that the "fat" he had been talking about stood for Faithful, Available, and Teachable. He told me that we need FAT people involved in the ministry. What a great thought! We most certainly do need FAT people in every area of life. Athletes need to be FAT. Coaches need to be FAT. Pastors need to be FAT. And the list goes on and on. The question now is...are you FAT?

Are you faithful to your team? Your family? Your Lord? Are you available to help, serve, or even listen? Are you teachable in your sport? At your school? In your walk with Christ? Are you FAT? As for me, well, I looked in the mirror today, and while I am working on being less fat in stature, I hope to always be FAT in Christ. My advice: Supersize it! Go large! Make it a Biggie size! Just be FAT for Christ! He needs you to be faithful, available, and teachable for His purposes and His glory.

GO:

1. Where do you struggle in being faithful, available, and teachable?

2. How have you put Jesus first in your life so that you can become FAT in Him?

3. Today, where can you be more FAT in Christ?

WORKOUT:

Psalm 119:30
Proverbs 14:6
Ephesians 3:20

I was a young lady obsessed with volleyball. I dreamed about it all the time. I constantly had a ball in my hands and was always doing approaches and rolls in the house. My dream was to play in college on a scholarship, and that dream came true when I was recruited as a setter at a Division II college in Missouri. I was very proud of myself, to say the least. I worked very hard the summer before my freshman year; I was in the best shape of my life and ready to begin the battle to earn a starting position. I did indeed believe I could start as a freshman if I worked hard enough and practiced long hours.

It began well, and I was starting games—but things changed as we lost matches. My coach began to implode, and she took out the losses on her players. (I was a big target because I was the setter). She was brutal with her language and imposed mental anguish and negativity with constant berating and blame-shifting. I cannot even begin to tell you the number of times that I called home and talked about quitting.

Now as I reflect on those days, I realize that not only was my volleyball dream not playing out as I had imagined, but college life in general was taking a toll on me. I was away from

DISAPPOINTMENTS

BY STEFANIE OTTO

home for the first time, and I found myself surrounded by an environment of few morals and many temptations. However, I was making friends, and I loved the college scene. Satan was doing his best to gain a victory over my life. I focused on Romans 12:2: "Do not conform any longer to the pattern of this world, but be transformed by the renewing of your mind. Then you will be able to test and approve what God's will is—his good, pleasing and perfect will" (NIV).

A family crisis at home caused me to leave the college I loved and all the great friends I had made. I know now that it was the Lord silently leading me out of a place not right for me as a follower of Jesus. Leaving was the right thing to do, so I moved back home to live with my parents at the end of the semester. I knew I had to find a way to get my love for volleyball back into my heart while at the same time keeping my mind renewed in Jesus.

I prayed a lot, and I know my parents did also. I attended a Bible-based church and renewed my Christian walk. After a year and half at the local junior college, I was blessed with another college scholarship at a Division II school in Minnesota. Once again I was recruited as a setter and planned on challenging another player for the starting spot. I knew I would do it, because I was successful at everything I did. I was granted the starting job for the first match of the season, but just before we were about to go out and warm up, my coach pulled me aside and told me that they were going to let the other setter start instead. I was devastated, and I questioned what I felt was injustice. Didn't I practice harder and give more effort? I knew that God was challenging my character. I am thankful that my parents were there to encourage me. I had to pull it together and be an example of courage to all the girls on my team no matter what position I was playing—even if it was the bench.

It took a lot of mental preparation for me to get to that point, as I continued to play on and off during the season. I focused on being unselfish and learned the hard way how to be a team player. I'm thankful for the Word of God which always teaches and exhorts. I had to constantly remind myself that God says, "Do not be anxious about anything, but in everything, by prayer and petition, with thanksgiving, present your requests to God. And the peace of God, which transcends all understanding, will guard your hearts and your minds in Christ Jesus" (Philippians 4:6–7 NIV). I ended the season having not played much and wondered what my senior season might bring. I questioned the wisdom of leaving Missouri, where I was assured of always being the starter.

Of course I wanted to be the star setter and leader of the team. Our team was ranked in the top twenty in the nation. I had always been successful, and taking second place was a hard road. As my senior year progressed, I came to the realization that I would not be setting. I did not want to be on the bench, either. After many nights of prayers and talks with my coaches, we decided that I would become a defensive specialist in the middle back of the court. It was a brand-new position for me. I had played left and right back, but never middle back. I was willing to do whatever my coaches wanted, just so I could be on the court. My pride had been honed

DISAPPOINTMENTS
BY STEFANIE OTTO

by God's circumstances, and even though it was hard, the thought of playing salved the harsh reality.

I must say that as I went through all those transitions, I found it very challenging to stay positive and switch my thought process to one of just doing my very best in all circumstances even if it was not initially what I had dreamed of doing. I had to trust that God was molding me to be the person *He* wanted me to be.

I had always wanted to be a volleyball coach, even when I was playing during high school. In all circumstances, I took mental notes of the kind of coach I wanted to be—and not to be. Looking back, I truly believe that God put me in three different colleges, each with different lessons, for a reason. I learned a great deal—both good and bad—from all three circumstances. I am still learning as a coach. Every season I grow to trust God more and more. No matter what happens to me, life's trials have taught me that God has my best interests in mind even if it hurts me emotionally for a while.

Philippians 4:13 says, "I can do everything through him who gives me strength" (NIV). I often think back on my young days as an athlete and realize that the "injustice" I thought I suffered was in reality God showing me His special love for me. James 1:12 says, "Blessed is the man who perseveres under trial, because when he has stood the test, he will receive the crown of life that God has promised to those who love him" (NIV).

Stefanie Otto is a top volleyball coach in Illinois. She has led her team to the state finals numerous times, but Coach Otto's yearly goal is to share her faith with her players so that they know where she stands with Christ.

The Rebekah Principle

READY:

"The servant hurried to meet her and said, 'Please give me a little water from your jar.' 'Drink, my lord,' she said, and quickly lowered the jar to her hands and gave him a drink. After she had given him a drink, she said, 'I'll draw water for your camels too, until they have finished drinking' " (Genesis 24:17–19 NIV).

SET:

Becky was the best player on her team. Everyone wanted to play like Becky. She was a hard worker, but there was more to her than what people could see. During a road trip, the last freshman selected for the team that year broke her foot during a practice before a game. When they arrived at the hotel that night, Becky carried her teammate's bags to her own room and asked her to stay with her. For the rest of the trip, Becky helped this little freshman with everything she needed.

Abraham was looking for the right woman for his son, Isaac. He sent a servant back to his homeland to find such a person. The servant prayed to find just the right woman, and along came Rebekah. Not only did Rebekah give him a drink, but also she took care of his camels. Ten camels that could drink about twenty gallons apiece would take about two hours to satisfy. This was the answer to the servant's prayer. Rebekah was the right one. Rebekah went the extra mile for this servant out of kindness, not duty. The "Rebekah Principle" is simple: Go the extra mile for someone today. Help someone who could use a hand.

Back to our story. Becky's other teammates could not understand why their top player would serve a freshman, but Becky did not care what her teammates thought about what she was doing. Becky understood that God calls us to serve, not to be served. She lived to serve God and knew that God would want her to help this teammate in need.

Are you applying the Rebekah Principle in your life today? Or are you applying minimal effort for a maximum return? God wants our *all*, freely given without expectation for anything in return. If you apply the Rebekah Principle in your life, the return for your investment will have an eternal reward!

GO:

1. To whom do you need to apply the Rebekah Principle in your life?

2. When have you done minimal work for the hope of a maximum return?

3. Today, how can you serve God better by serving others?

WORKOUT:

Mark 10:42–45
Ephesians 6:7–8
Philippians 2:3

What Stinks?

"Whatever is true, whatever is noble, whatever is right, whatever is pure, whatever is lovely, whatever is admirable—if anything is excellent or praiseworthy—think about such things" (Philippians 4:8 NIV).

I had a point guard who struggled early on with her play and her self-confidence. After beating herself up after a practice, I stood by her and said, "What stinks?" She replied, "My game." I disagreed and said it was her attitude about her game. I told her to stop her "stinkin' thinkin' "!

Too many times we tend to think the worst about ourselves or our situations. We tend to find our value in who we are as athletes, not who we are with Christ. When this happens, as it did with this player, our stinkin' thinkin' takes over and our God-pleasing thoughts take a backseat.

Paul reminds us in Philippians that we need to think about things that are noble, right, pure, lovely, admirable, and praiseworthy! Our lives are meant to be pleasing to God. We honor God when we think good things— not bad things. Too much of life is caught up in the negative. Let's focus on the positive for God's glory.

Later in the year, my team was down at the half and playing terribly. After a less-than-positive halftime talk, my team slowly walked out of the locker room and back to the court to warm up. The last player to pass me was this young point guard. She said to

100

me, "Coach, stop your stinkin' thinkin', 'cause we ain't losing this game!" You know what? She was right. We won! It's good to practice what we preach, but I will save that for another devotional. Let's quit our stinkin' thinkin' and start our positive thinking for kingdom-living!

GO:

1. How often does your attitude carry a less-than-desirable smell?

2. Have you focused much on Philippians 4:8 before?

3. How can you stop your stinkin' thinkin' and start kingdom-living today?

WORKOUT:

Proverbs 15:26
Mark 7:20–22
Psalm 139:16–18

True Worship

"Shout it aloud, do not hold back. Raise your voice like a trumpet. Declare to my people their rebellion and to the house of Jacob their sins. For day after day they seek me out; they seem eager to know my ways, as if they were a nation that does what is right and has not forsaken the commands of its God. They ask me for just decisions and seem eager for God to come near them. 'Why have we fasted,' they say, 'and you have not seen it? Why have we humbled ourselves, and you have not noticed?' " (Isaiah 58:1–3 NIV).

SET:

I know a team that loves to talk the talk but doesn't know how to walk the walk. They look the part, but many of them do not work for the true good of the team. Many are in it just for the status and the look, thinking that they have already arrived. On game day, they are dressed to the hilt. They say the right things and look the part, but when the ball is in play, you find out what they are truly made of and how much they have really prepared themselves for the competition.

Isaiah knew a group of people just like that. They thought they had it going on—putting on their spiritual airs in public. But in private, their lives were totally different. Sure, they fasted and went through the spiritual motions, but that didn't get them very far. Isaiah warned them that going through the motions wouldn't cut it! Living the Christian life is more than punching the time clock at church, FCA, or weekly Bible studies. It is a 24/7 commitment to living, learning, and loving

God and knowing Him more. We are fooling and cheating ourselves by doing anything less than that. Is it easy? Absolutely not. It requires work. Only in the dictionary does success come *before* work. Growing in Christ and truly worshipping Him takes work on your part. Commitment is the key. God wants you to truly worship Him, not practice false or pious worship just to make yourself look the part.

This team I mentioned earlier has great potential. There are great leaders within, but they need to find out what it means to work together in order to reach the highest goal in their sport. Will they be able to show that they have done what it takes as individuals *and* the whole, or will they show that they don't know how to walk the walk? Will their lack of work come out in their performances on the field? I am looking forward to finding out. Time will tell. More importantly, as followers of Christ, are we just talking the talk and putting on our spiritual clothes for Sunday? Make a decision today to evaluate your spiritual walk and then walk it! No one wants to follow an idle talker!

GO:

1. How would you describe your work, play, and worship?

2. Are you a talker or a walker?

3. How can you improve your walk with Christ today?

WORKOUT:

John 4:23–24
1 Corinthians 15:58
Hebrews 12:28–29

God's Playbook

"Direct my footsteps according to your word; let no sin rule over me" (Psalm 119:133 NIV).

Most sports have a playbook or set of rules to follow in their program—something that tells how things will be done on and off the field for success in the system. I recently heard one coach refer to his playbook as his "bible." Obviously, he highly values the book.

As we read through Psalm 119, we find many verses that reference God's Word. Although David appears to be one if not *the* main contributor of the book of Psalms, it is actually a compilation of writings from several authors—yet even among this varied authorship, we find it repeated many times that God's Word guided the writer. They understood that God's Word was the only playbook they could follow that could give true, absolute direction for life.

When I coached basketball, my playbook was very important to me. However, it did not take precedence over the real Playbook of my life. Only God's Word can give ultimate direction. My basketball playbook could say which play to run in what situation, but only during the games. God's Word gives us direction every day, for every situation, in everything that comes our way.

GO:

1. Where do you go for direction?

2. Does God's Word guide your steps, or are you marching to a different beat?

3. How can you start to make the Bible your ultimate road map today?

WORKOUT:

Psalm 119:11, 73, 105

Fear Factor

"Now this is what the LORD says—the One who created you, Jacob, and the One who formed you, Israel—'Do not fear, for I have redeemed you; I have called you by your name; you are Mine' " (Isaiah 43:1 HCSB).

SET:

Jeff stepped up to the plate. The bases were loaded with two outs, and his team was down by one run. You could tell he was nervous. How would Jeff respond? *Strike one!* He watched it go by. *Strike two!* He watched another. *Strike three!* The bat never left Jeff's shoulder. Jeff returned to the dugout and was approached by his coach. "You never even took a swing. Why not?" Jeff replied, "I thought you would be mad if I struck out swinging."

This happens a lot in sports. Fear grips an athlete. Fear of a coach, fear of failure, fear of losing... Whatever the fear may be, fear is a factor in sports today—and in life, as well.

In many Christian homes across the country, fear is being taught. And not the good kind of respectful fear, but the kind that can make a person timid and afraid. Faith can become so legalistic that fear grips the hearts of young and old. Christ did not come to earth to instill fear but to give freedom from it. Pastors may preach fear and parents may instill fear, because, after all, being fearful is not necessarily a bad thing. But Christ does not intend for us to live in fear. He intends for us to live in the freedom that we can find in Him.

What fear grips your life? Maybe it is the fear of not being forgiven. Maybe it's the fear that God's grace is not enough for you or the fear that God's love does not include you. *Fear not*, friends. Just as good coaches do not intend to make their players fearful of them, God also does not intend for you to live in fear—but in freedom from sin and death by living for Him. Fear does not need to be a factor in your athletic world or in your life with Christ. Remember, He has called you, and you are His forever.

GO:

1. What do you fear when you compete? In what ways could a coach cause you fear?

2. How do you have freedom from sin in your life?

3. How can you start today to live free from fear as a child of God?

WORKOUT:

Jeremiah 29:11–14
Daniel 10:19
Hebrews 13:6

Whatever

"Finally brothers, whatever is true, whatever is honorable, whatever is just, whatever is pure, whatever is lovely, whatever is commendable—if there is any moral excellence and if there is any praise—dwell on these things" (Philippians 4:8 HCSB).

SET:

Sometime in the 90s, one word became popular not only in the world of sports, but in American culture. This word drove me nuts as a coach. My players and especially my student secretary would use this word constantly. "Whatever, Coach," they'd say while rolling their eyes. When they didn't want to hear what I had to say or didn't agree with me, they would drop the "W bomb," as I called it. When I hear that word today, it can still bring me to an uncomfortable state of mind.

Paul, however, uses the word in a much different way. He challenges us to fix our thoughts on six things that can bring glory to Christ: truth, honor, justice, purity, loveliness, and commendable acts or deeds. These are the thought patterns that should consume our minds. All these things come from God and are a part of His Son's life. Jesus was true, honorable, just, pure, lovely, and commendable, and we should be giving Him praise and dwelling on Him, don't you think?

Now whenever I hear the word *whatever* come out a person's mouth, I immediately go to Philippians 4:8 for encouragement instead of letting it frustrate me. Whatever is in store for your day today, make it true, honorable, just, pure, lovely, and commendable. This will bring proper glory to the One who deserves all honor and glory. Whatever you are about today, be about Christ! Remember, whatever fills our minds will come out eventually.

GO:

1. On what are you fixing your mind today?

2. How can focusing on these six things encourage your positive thinking this week?

3. Today, how can you fix your mind on the things of God?

WORKOUT:

John 8:14
Romans 1:17
2 Corinthians 7:11
1 Timothy 3:8

Didn't See It Coming

READY:

"Then the LORD opened the donkey's mouth...."
(Numbers 22:28 NIV).

SET:

John was a great miler. He always liked to take the lead early in the race and run to victory. His coach, however, was concerned about an upcoming race. John's top opponent was one who liked to come from behind to win.

When the event started, John raced to the lead like clockwork. His coach told him to move to the inside of lane one, but John ignored him. He liked to run in the first lane, but not always on the inside. On laps two and three his coach said the same thing, and John grew upset with him. John knew he had the lead—the victory was his. On lap four, his coach became more insistent that John move to the inside of the lane, but John stayed firm in the middle.

In the Old Testament, Balaam had a similar situation with his faithful donkey. Balaam was traveling down the road on his donkey, but God sent an angel to oppose Balaam, as He was angry with him. The donkey could see the angel, although Balaam could not. The donkey moved to avoid the angel, and Balaam became angry and hit his donkey.

Three times the donkey avoided the angel, who was sent to strike down Balaam, and Balaam hit his faithful steed every time. Finally God opened the donkey's mouth, and she and Balaam had a conversation. Now, if my donkey started talking to me, I'd certainly take notice, but Balaam was so blinded by his anger that he did not listen. God had to open Balaam's eyes to see what the donkey had saved him from receiving. Balaam repented of his sin and turned to God for forgiveness.

On the final turn of his race, John stayed firmly in his chosen position. In the last ten yards, his opponent passed him on the inside and took the victory. John's coach had seen what John himself could not. He knew John's opponent was coming on strong and that if John did not move to the inside, he would be beaten. John, like Balaam, had a blind spot and could not see what was coming.

Many times we do not listen to others who want to show us areas of improvement because we cannot see the need ourselves. We all have blind spots. But pay attention. God may be using others to show you what you need to change today.

GO:

1. What are the blind spots in your life as an athlete and a Christian?

2. Who has helped you to see your blind spots?

3. How can you eliminate your spiritual blind spots?

WORKOUT:

Proverbs 12:15
Proverbs 13:10
Proverbs 15:22

The Day My World Changed

On June 17, 1996, my life was forever changed. On that awesome day, my brown-eyed beauty was born. From the first moment that our eyes locked, she stole my heart. And as each year passes, my love and amazement of her grows.

My name is Derwin L. Gray, but you can call me "Dewey." I played five years in the NFL with the Indianapolis Colts (1993–1997) and one year with the Carolina Panthers (1998). I am now a pastor at a church called theGathering. I also write books and travel around the country, speaking at various events and sharing the love of Christ. My many years of football experience have enabled me to appear as a guest analyst for *Fox Charlotte TV* and *ESPNU*. God in His grace has gifted me with the capabilities to do many things, but the single greatest gift He has given me is the chance to be a husband and a father. Writing this with my daughter, Presley, means so much!

Hi, my name is Presley, and I am in seventh grade. I have a newfound love with an awesome sport: cheerleading. It teaches me teamwork, patience, and understanding, and I can use those things at home with my family. I love spending time with my dad, or *Papi*, as I call him. He's really funny and outgoing. We share almost all the same interests, too! We both love seafood, we're both creative—and we both dislike math. My father and I want to share with you some spiritual exercises that will help you to "get real" with Jesus.

Spiritual Exercises

Prayer. Prayer is not about approaching God with a wish list, like a five-year-old would a parent during the Christmas season. God already knows what you need (Matthew 6:32). Prayer is about face-to-face intimacy with our heavenly "Papi." It is a conversation and a meeting place between two friends. Prayer is where we release our fears and burdens, ask questions, and listen to God. Prayer is not a scheduled once-a-day appointment during our "quiet time." It is an ongoing, abiding dialogue with God as we practice His presence in all of life's activities.

Feasting on the Word of God. As a football player, I knew that if I studied my playbook, I could play better in the games because I would know what I was doing. When I became one of God's athletes, I realized that God gave His players a playbook called the Bible. So I committed to reading it and embracing its teaching. Soon I realized that the more I read God's Playbook, the more God fed my soul with Himself. I experienced why He is called the Bread of Life (John 6:35).

All of life is worship. As God's athletes, all of life is sacred (1 Corinthians 10:31)! The only thing that is not sacred is sin.

GET REAL WITH GOD

Whether you are getting busy in the big game, studying for a huge exam, going to the movies, or even when you are on a date, you carry the Father, the Son, and the Holy Spirit with you if you have given your life to Christ! All of life is sacred ground because the sacred God lives in you. It is a spiritual exercise to remember this awesome reality. As you practice it, watch how you begin to see all of life differently. Even the most mundane things can become worship...even taking a algebra exam!

"Solitude and silence." We live in a loud, distracting world. Solitude simply means finding a quiet place away from our iPhones, computers, iPods, TVs, and even sometimes other people, just to be with God in complete silence. It is vital that you occasionally take time away from the noise to unplug. If you do not intentionally pull away from distractions, then distractions will pull you away from getting real with God and His great plans for your life.

Community. You need people, and people need you. When you first embraced Jesus, He brought you, an individual, into His kingdom for the purpose of integrating you into His family of disciples. You are a first-round draft pick on the ultimate team, the Church. You need people in your life who will encourage you—and you need people in your life that you can encourage. Get plugged into a local church if you've not already found one.

Witnessing and Serving. You have what the world needs— hope. Hope for forgiveness. Hope for emotional healing. And hope for life after death. Jesus has given you the Good

GETTING IN SHAPE
BY DERWIN AND PRESLEY GRAY

News to share. Share it through the way you allow *Him* to live through you in service to others. As you display Jesus' second greatest commandment to the Pharisees (Matthew 22:36–40) by the way you serve people, they will begin to ask you why you do what you do. At that moment, you can humbly share the Good News with them. And remember that it is more important to talk to God about people than it is to talk to people about God. Pray for your Christless friends and be ready to share the Good News with them.

Presley and I will be praying for you. Let's get in shape!

Much love,
Derwin & Presley

Former NFL player Derwin L. Gray is also known as "The Evangelism Linebacker." He is the pastor of preaching and spiritual formation of "theGathering," a multi-ethnic, intergenerational equipping church in Charlotte, North Carolina. He also serves as the president of One Heart at a Time Ministries. Learn more at www.oneheartatatime.org. Derwin's first book, *Hero*, will be releasing in September 2009 from Summerside Press. Derwin lives in North Carolina with his wife, Vicki, and their two children, Presley and Jeremiah.

Proper Preparation

"After fasting forty days and forty nights, he [Jesus] was hungry" (Matthew 4:2 NIV).

How do you prepare for a game? For a season? For a test? Do you spend time making a game plan that will work, or do you just hope for the best? While watching teams play over the years in many different sports, one begins to wonder. Some teams work their plans to perfection, but you wonder if others just roll out the balls in practice while the coach takes a nap. Now, we know that never happens; preparing for a contest or upcoming season takes much time in being devoted to the necessary details before a team is ready to compete. Then it comes—the final day before the games begin. Will the team be able to put into practice what they worked so hard at perfecting? Physically, they may be ready, but what about mentally, or better yet, spiritually? Spiritually prepared? Yes—God does care how you prepare to compete and perform in action and in attitude.

Jesus Himself had to prepare for battle and competition, even though His foe was no match. Before Jesus began His earthly ministry, He was led into the wilderness by the Holy Spirit to be tempted by Satan. In order to prepare, Jesus ate nothing for forty days and nights. What a game plan! Jesus knew His task. He studied

116

and knew his opponent well. He took away any distractions that could possibly hinder His singular focus for His life. By fasting in preparation for His work on earth, Jesus focused solely on following God's plan for His life. Even though the temptation to follow other plans was given immediately after His time of fasting and preparation, He was steadfast and true, showing not only that He truly was the Son of God, but that true strength and spiritual readiness come only from the Father in heaven!

As you prepare to play, I am certainly not suggesting that you fast for forty days and nights, but I am suggesting that you follow Christ's example by being prepared spiritually for competition so you'll be able to withstand the testing and trials of life and sport. Will you follow the game plan of the team to the end or give in when the first trial or temptation comes along?

GO:

1. What is one weak area of your preparation?

2. Do you consider it important to be spiritually ready to compete?

3. What can you do to better prepare for competing in sport and life?

WORKOUT:

Ephesians 6:10–18
2 Timothy 4:2

I Am a
C-H-R-I-S-T-I-A-N

"Rejoice in the Lord always; again I will say, Rejoice"
(Philippians 4:4 ESV).

Tuesday is always trash day. And on some Tuesdays, there seems
to be very little good about the morning. Daily tasks often can
become mundane, but not on this particular day. Every Tuesday
morning I am the member of the family who deposits the trash
into the proper container. This morning, as I sat back at the table
lamenting the fact that I had to take the trash out to the curb, I
heard a song resonating from an upstairs bedroom. "I am C...I am
C-H...I am a C-H-R-I-S-T-I-A-N." It was coming from my seven-
year-old, who was joyfully ringing in the day.

Rejoice... Now there's a word we don't use every day. The
word *rejoice* basically means "full of joy." In your line of work
in business or your role as a student or coach, do you
ever get lost in what you *do* rather than who you *are*?
I know that, for myself, when I struggle with what I
do, my rejoicing in Christ is not what it should be.
The verse above, however, reminds us that we are to
rejoice in every situation (always) for who we are
in Christ instead of worrying about what we do
from day to day.

Today I was the trash man.
Tomorrow I may be a baseball coach.
The next day, possibly the yard
man. But every day I am a C...

118

I am a C-H...I am a C-H-R-I-S-T-I-A-N! What about you? Whatever your role is today, don't forget who you are. You are a dearly loved child of God—a Christ-follower. We are people who love the Lord with all our hearts, so let's be filled with joy like my little seven-year-old was this morning. Last night he was a pitcher; this morning he was the tired son. But every day he knows in his little heart what and who he truly is: a CHRISTIAN!

So what do you say? Maybe it's time to be full of joy and not ashamed to let people know it.

GO:

1. How do you wake up to attack your day? Are you full of joy or something else?

2. How easy is it for you to get caught up in what you do rather than who you are?

3. What can you do to remind yourself of the joy you have in being a follower of Christ?

WORKOUT:

Psalm 118:24
Mark 12:30
Luke 9:23

All Ears

"Pay close attention to my words; let this be the consolation you offer" (Job 21:2 HCSB).

SET:

Sarah was struggling on her team. She just couldn't get her game together. She went from starting to sitting the bench, and then she tore her ACL in practice. After having surgery to repair her knee, Sarah was visited at her house by her three best friends. Sarah started to share her frustration, but each time she did, she was interrupted by her friends telling her what she should have done to avoid the injury. Sarah became even more frustrated.

Job was in a similar situation. He had everything going for him until the day Satan was allowed to take everything from him. Job was extremely discouraged and was lamenting his lot in life to God when three friends came by to visit. When Job started to speak, his friends didn't seem to listen. Each friend told Job what was wrong—that God had put him in his horrible situation. Finally, Job said to them that he would rather they listen to him, which would help him more, rather than try to tell him what they thought he'd done wrong.

Like Sarah, many athletes who struggle would rather have someone listen to them share their frustrations than trying to tell them their opinion. Such is the case with people who are struggling in life. Listening may give you the opportunity to share God's good news down the road. Speaking too quickly could bring frustration and anger instead. Learn to listen first. You may not even have to speak to make someone's day.

GO:

1. Are you a good listener?

2. Are you always quick to respond, or can you hold your tongue once in a while?

3. How can you be a better listener for your friends?

WORKOUT:

Proverbs 18:13
James 1:19

Be a David

READY:

"David said to Saul, 'Don't let anyone be discouraged by him; your servant will go and fight this Philistine!' " (1 Samuel 17:32 HCSB).

SET:

Competitive toughness is something all athletes strive for. Tennis legend Chris Evert once said, "Competitive toughness is an acquired skill, not an inherited gift." The ability to be mentally and physically tough in sports today is something that athletes have to work for daily. Just because your parents may have been great athletes does not mean you will be. You have to work on it.

The Bible's David developed competitive toughness as a young boy. He watched the family's flock of sheep, fended off lions and bears, and endured a long stretch of patience when he wanted to fight in battle but was not allowed. When David finally got his chance, however, he was ready. He willingly took on a massive warrior and won. He was not afraid of Goliath because he knew he could defeat him. The Lord was with David, and David had that edge to help him.

As the described "man after God's own heart," David's example can teach us many things from both in and beyond his bout with Goliath. In fact, we should all be Davids when it comes to certain areas.

1. Courageously defend your flock against the lions and bears of the world.
2. Be willing to fight the Goliaths in life, one stone at a time.
3. Be a loyal friend no matter what the situation.

122

4. Be ready to lead, regardless of your age or status.
5. Face your failures and own up to them.
6. Never take forgiveness lightly or a blessing for granted.
7. Learn from your mistakes.
8. Strive to develop trust and faith in your teammates.
9. Create an unchangeable belief in God's faithfulness.
10. Chase success, but pursue God's heart.

We can learn a lot from David's successes and failures, and I would encourage you to read about his entire life when you have the time so that you can fully understand each point on the list above. However, we can summarize "being a David" by loving God, loving others, and loving life. Be tough, be competitive, be a Christian in the midst of the battle, and be a David—after God's own heart.

GO:

1. When do you feel tough in your sport?

2. In what spiritual areas do you need to get tougher?

3. Today, how can you be a David in the midst of life's daily grind?

WORKOUT:

1 Samuel 17
1 Timothy 6:12
1 Timothy 4:7

Worry Less

"Anxiety in a man's heart weighs it down, but a good word cheers it up" (Proverbs 12:25 HCSB).

SET:

Okay, I admit it. I worry too much. I worry about work, worry about my family, worry, worry, worry. And it seems like for every worry I have, I gain ten pounds. Talk about being weighed down! And we all struggle with it from time to time.

So how do we get rid of the baggage that worry brings? Well, that's easy—leave it at the cross. Which, as we all know, is easier said than done. However, the second part of today's verse is quite helpful. When I tend to worry too much, I find myself encouraging others more. I love to encourage others and brighten their days. Encouragement is fuel to our lives. It keeps our tanks full and overflowing.

Worry is a habit, and a bad one at that. Not only is it a bad habit, but we're commanded in scripture not to do it (see the Matthew verses below). Encouragement, on the other hand, is a good habit. My advice today: Worry less, encourage more. It's always good to receive encouragement, but don't wait for it before you start giving it out. Make it a point today to encourage ten people. Trust me, it is contagious. But so is worrying. So keep in mind as you either encourage or worry that your actions not only affect you but others around you, too.

Today, for the sake of

yourselves and others, worry less and encourage more! What are you waiting for?

GO:

1. Do you worry too much?
2. Do you encourage others enough?
3. Today, how can you start to worry less and encourage more?

WORKOUT:

Proverbs 12
Matthew 6:25–34

Running on the Edge

"Mark out a straight path for your feet; stay on the safe path" (Proverbs 4:26 NLT).

SET:

Driving down the road recently, I saw something that made me take notice. Coming toward me was a middle-aged man running against the traffic. Now, that did not bother me so much; I see that all the time. But what I found strange was that he had on his iPod and was running right along the edge of the cars. Not ten feet from him on his left was a beautiful, well-groomed sidewalk, on which there was not a single person. I couldn't help but break out into laughter.

After I stopped laughing, God spoke to me. "What's so funny?" I felt Him asking. "You do that all the time." I respectfully replied, "I do not. I don't even run anymore." Okay, it's probably not a great idea to get sarcastic with the Creator of the world. I knew where He was going. He reminded me of the sin in my life and how many times I run, walk, and live on the edge of sin when He (the Creator of the perfect path) has given me a clear and safe sidewalk.

Why is it that we, like this iPoded man, run in harm's way on the edge of sin? Maybe we think we can stay on the edge and never go over it. But Satan, the creator of all sin, does not play fair, and he will do anything he can to bring us to the brink of destruction. Proverbs 4:26

tells us to mark out a straight path for our feet and stay on the safe path—the path God intends for us.

What is running on the edge to you? Maybe it is the party everyone goes to after the game, being alone with your boyfriend, or staying up late and watching something questionable on TV. I don't know what the edge is for you, but you do! Running on the sidewalk of life may not be appealing, but it is the safest place to be. God provides us with a safe path. Our job is to run, walk, and live in it.

GO:

1. When was the last time you were running on life's edge?

2. What are those areas in your life that tend to drag you to the edge?

3. How can you run, walk, and live on the safe path with Christ daily?

WORKOUT:

Psalm 1:6
Proverbs 4:27
1 Corinthians 10:13

Getting Cut: A Good Thing?

READY:

"And we know that in all things God works for the good of those who love him, who have been called according to his purpose" (Romans 8:28 NIV).

SET:

By the third preseason game of an NFL team, many players find out where they stand in trying to make the cut. One such player, Jason, found out some bad news. Before his third game, he was told that he had been cut. Jason drove home, obviously disappointed in not making the team.

At times we don't understand why God does the things He does. We try to follow Him and do right by Him, but when things don't go our way, we question Him. But with God, when He closes a door to something *we* think would be great for us, it means that *He* has something much better in store for us. It's hard at times to wait for answers as to why things don't work out, but God will provide the knowledge in due time. As Paul states in Romans, God causes *everything* to work for the good of those who love and follow Him.

Not long after he got home that day, Jason received a phone call from a friend. Joe, Jason's friend, asked to meet him at a local club to talk, and Jason agreed. When he arrived at the club, Jason listened to Joe's compelling story. Until recently, Joe had never been to church, owned a Bible, or recognized that God was in control. But while driving around one day, something happened that Joe couldn't understand. He felt a presence in his car and heard a voice telling him, "It's time, Joe, to follow Me." Joe didn't know who to turn to except his friend Jason. Jason spent the next several hours in the club sharing his faith with Joe. At two in the morning, Joe became a follower of Jesus Christ.

Why was Jason cut from the team? I don't know. But I do know that if he had made the team, he would not have been available to meet with Joe. God used Jason even during a tough time in his life to bring glory to His name. Jason was a faithful, available servant. Because Jason was cut another person came to the throne of God and started a personal relationship with Christ.

When the bad things in life cause you to doubt, hold on. God's got something good coming your way. Make sure you are ready and available.

GO:

1. How often do you question why God does what He does?

2. How can you start waiting on God for answers in your spiritual journey?

3. Today, how can you make sure you're ready and available?

WORKOUT:

Proverbs 3:5–6
Jeremiah 29:11
1 Peter 5:6

I grew up in a wonderful family with six brothers and five sisters. My mom and dad were amazing, loving, and very caring parents. I learned the values of hard work and perseverance from them. I am so thankful to be from a large family. My brothers and sisters are my best friends.

South Dakota State University, where I attended, played, and lettered in four different sports, had a tremendous Fellowship of Christian Athletes program. I went to those FCA meetings on occasion. There was such a presence of the Lord there, which I could not define then but recognize now. I was always so glad I went. The students who went seemed to have a genuineness about them that others on campus never portrayed (even myself). Even though I was experiencing a good amount of success on my teams and in the classroom, there was a real emptiness in my heart. I was searching for something "real," but I didn't know what I was in search of.

There were three questions in my heart I didn't have answers for: (1) *Who am I?* Even though I knew my name and the wonderful family I was a part of, I often wondered who

IDENTITY CRISIS
BY TANYA CREVIER

I really was; (2) *Where am I going to go when I die?* My family and I went to church faithfully, and I knew about God, believed in Him, and knew that Jesus had died on the cross for my sins. I still had no assurance of my faith and what my faith in Jesus Christ represented and did for me; (3) *What am I going to do for the rest of my life?* I knew there had to be more to life than just "going to school," "getting a job," etc. *What am I here on this earth to do? Who am I to live my life for?*

I had no answers for these questions and wondered if I ever would. My brother Marc was talking with me one day, and he seemed to have some of the answers I was looking for. As he started sharing Bible verses with me, the Word of God was speaking to my heart: "Jesus told him, 'I am the way, the truth, and the life. No one can come to the Father except through me' " (John 14:6 NLT). First John 5:11–13 reads, "This is the testimony: God has given us eternal life, and this life is in His Son. The one who has the Son has life. The one who doesn't have the Son of God does not have life. I have written these things to you who believe in the name of the Son of God, so that you may know that you have eternal life" (HCSB).

After hearing these verses and others, I knew then and there that I needed to accept Jesus Christ into my heart and make him "real" in my life. John 1:12 says, "But to all who did receive Him, who believed in his name, he gave the right to become children of God" (ESV). My brother led me in a prayer of faith upon my believing that Jesus Christ did for me what I couldn't do for myself—forgive me of my sins, by

His blood. I accepted His forgiveness and, by faith, Him into my heart. At this point Jesus became "real" to me. He now lives in my heart, and I know that!

Now all of my questions are answered by trusting Jesus Christ as my Savior: (1) I am now a child of God; (2) I know I will spend eternity in heaven with Jesus. He is preparing a place for me. I belong to Him; (3) My goal now is to "Let your light shine before others, so that they may see your good works and give glory to your Father who is in heaven" (Matthew 5:16 ESV).

God has blessed me with a unique talent of spinning, juggling, and dribbling basketballs. I am invited to perform my skills at many different venues: schools, basketball camps, prisons, basketball games, and even nursing homes. Now, as I am invited to share my skills, I know the importance of communicating the love of God to others as I am given the platform through sports.

Jesus Christ and the Holy Spirit keeps me going strong for the glory of God and His honor every day. God's Word (the Bible) is now my playbook. Jesus is my coach, and I am directed through life each day by the power of the Holy Spirit.

Tanya Crevier is a world-famous basketball ball handler. She has traveled the globe, sharing her message in schools, NBA games, and prison ministry. Tanya's passion is sharing how the Lord changed her heart and passing it along to as many people as she can. Tanya can be contacted through www.enthusiasminternational.com or at tanya@ enthusiasminternational.com.

IDENTITY CRISIS
BY TANYA CREVIER

Practice, Practice, Practice

"Proclaim the message; persist in it whether convenient or not; rebuke, correct, and encourage with great patience and teaching" (2 Timothy 4:2 HCSB).

I love to golf. I used to be fairly good. Well, kind of good. Okay, just average. But I love to play! The thing I don't like about golf is practicing. Hitting a couple of putts, swinging the club to loosen up, and then going out to play has been my golf routine in recent years. So why should I expect to be any good? Getting better at something takes practice, practice, and more practice. Golf is no exception. No wonder Tiger and Vijay are so good!

One thing Paul understood about sharing his faith was that it took practice, and lots of it! He was always ready to practice sharing on someone. He passed on his practice of sharing to Timothy. He instructed him to be ready to share his faith at all times. Practicing sharing your faith should be a privilege we look forward to instead of a torturous experience. And when we do share our faith, we need to make sure we know the details. Part of our practice time needs to be spent in studying God's Word to know what it says. God's Word always supersedes man's word. As much as I love golf, I will never improve without consistent practice. As we grow in Christ, sharing our faith will require more practice, too. The more we share our faith, the easier it will become. In the end, no matter how much I improve at golf, it doesn't measure up to the practice of sharing my faith with others. Today, start making it a daily habit to share about Christ. All that practice will pay off in the end.

GO:

1. Do you like to practice your sport?
2. When is the last time you shared your faith?
3. How can you begin the practice of sharing your faith with unbelievers?

WORKOUT:

Acts 6:4
1 Thessalonians 2:13
1 Peter 1:25

The Good, the Bad, and the Ugly

"Whatever happens, conduct yourselves in a manner worthy of the gospel of Christ" (Philippians 1:27 NIV).

Does this sound familiar? "The ref made me mad, so I had to say it!" Or maybe this one: "It's not my fault I got a tech; did you see what he did to me?" We've all been there. We've all let our attitudes and anger control our actions and achievements. Then we play the justification game. We've learned that it is never our fault but usually a teammate's, an opposing player's, or the coach's. When I coached, I was constantly reminded of how I acted in tough situations during the game with officials. Was I being Christlike in my walk and talk during the game? Many times I failed to reach the mark.

Paul was a great example of how to conduct oneself during tough times. Paul was beaten, thrown into jail, and almost killed on many occasions, but he constantly maintained an attitude of gratitude. He stated in Philippians that we need to conduct ourselves in a way that will honor Christ by what we do and say— no matter what happens.

So when things don't go your way, whether on or off the court, do you let your attitude control your altitude with Christ? Whatever happens, whether the good, bad, or ugly in life, make Jesus Christ proud of your response to the situation.

When your way doesn't work...
look to Yahweh!

GO:

1. When has your attitude affected your altitude with Christ?

2. When has your way gotten in the way of God's way for you?

3. Is your conduct worthy or worthless?

WORKOUT:

1 Thessalonians 4:1
Romans 14:12–13
Romans 6:11–13

Never Forget

"So his fame spread even to distant places, for he was marvelously helped until he became strong. But when he became strong, he grew arrogant and it led to his own destruction. He acted unfaithfully against the LORD his God by going into the LORD's sanctuary to burn incense on the incense altar" (2 Chronicles 26:15—16 HCSB).

We know them well. Athletes who, at first, worked hard and gave the credit to God for their success. But then as they became more and more successful, they gave God the glory less and less. We see it happen all the time—the once-humble athlete asking for more of the world and less of God. Their pride takes over!

King Uzziah was one of these men. Under the spiritual influence of Zechariah, Uzziah sought the Lord and was blessed in his pursuit of Him. This blessing was taken to heart—the wrong heart. Uzziah started to focus more on himself and less on what God had done for him. He quickly became powerful, and he just as quickly forgot what (or who) got him to that point. He even began ignoring his spiritual mentor. Who needed Zechariah? Uzziah was on top of the world! He became so proud and brash that he even entered the temple and tried to do things only the priests were allowed to do. Worshipping and serving God became all about him.

God has a way of bring people to their knees. Remember, pride always comes before a fall. Uzziah's fall began when his disobedience led to leprosy. This disease led to his spiritual and ultimate defeat. God reminded Uzziah every day through his leprosy, "Never forget, I am still *the* Man!"

Have you forgotten who the Man truly is? Too many of us today reek of pride! Don't forget you are only a fallen, broken human being restored by Christ. Only He is *the* Man. Never forget who created you and why He did it: so you would serve Him and live to glorify Him in all you do. Oh yeah, and give credit where credit is due...lest you break out with an unknown rash on your forehead.

GO:

1. What are you prideful about? When has pride taken over your life?

2. How can you remain humble?

3. How can you start to remember what God has done for you today?

WORKOUT:

2 Chronicles 26
Psalm 101:5
Proverbs 8:13; 11:2; 16:5, 18

What Do You Want from Me?

" 'And now, Israel, what does the LORD your God require of you? He requires only that you fear the LORD your God, and live in a way that pleases him, and love him and serve him with all your heart and soul. And you must always obey the LORD's commands and decrees that I am giving you today for your own good' " (Deuteronomy 10:12–13 NLT).

Michael had the potential to be a good player, but he got so frustrated with his game. He did not understand why his coach always wanted him to change his shot and other parts of his game. He finally had a talk with his coach, and things suddenly became clearer to him. His improvement took off. Coach simply told Michael what he needed to do to get better and how it would help him in years to come.

As Moses was leading the people of Israel through the wilderness, many started to grumble and complain. Though God continued to provide for their needs, they soon forgot His provisions. God gave Moses the guidelines to live by, and Moses constantly shared them with his people. I can picture someone approaching Moses and saying, "What does He [God] want from me?" Moses summarized God's desire with these verses in Deuteronomy, sharing four things: fear Him, live for Him, love Him, and serve Him. Everything we do is encompassed by these things.

Have you ever felt like Michael? I know I have, both athletically and spiritually. When I read these verses again, God opened my heart to understand them in a better way. If you are struggling with what God wants from you, spend some time in these verses, too. See where the Lord needs you to grow and get "One Day Better" in Him. I hope they will bless your heart as much as they recently have mine.

GO:

1. When was a time you struggled with what someone expected or required from you? What was the outcome?

2. How are you doing in the four areas indicated from today's verses?

3. Today, which of these four areas will you make a greater effort to grow in?

WORKOUT:

Mark 12:30–31
1 Thessalonians 4:1–3
Romans 14:12–13

The Most Important Thing

"But you will receive power when the Holy Spirit has come upon you, and you will be My witnesses in Jerusalem, in all Judea and Samaria, and to the ends of the earth" (Acts 1:8 HCSB).

SET:

There are so many important things to do before we get to heaven: get an education, stay fit and active, be part of a team, make quality friends, be a friend, and much, much more. We are so blessed to be able to live in this world and do the things we do—yet while reading Mark Cahill's book, *The One Thing You Can't Do in Heaven*, I have been reminded that I sometimes miss out on the most important thing that we're to do while here on earth, and that is to share our faith with others. The dreaded "E" word—evangelism. Many will say, "That is the pastor's job" or "I don't know what to say" or "They won't listen to me." Those may all be true statements, but it doesn't get us out of our responsibility as followers of Christ. One compelling statement Cahill makes in his book is, "Friends don't let friends go to hell." If we truly care about the ones we love, won't we naturally want to tell them about the most important thing in our life?

What I am realizing from day to day is that the things of this earth really don't mean a whole lot. Winning games, having new cars or the latest fashion trends—all of these are nice, but not one of them comes close to what we have in store for us someday with Christ. I'm not encouraging you to forget everything you have in this life, but don't forsake and forget about the *One* who gave life to you. One young man in Cahill's book said he wanted to be a Christian but still be cool. Cahill replied that going to heaven someday would be cool. Cahill went on to tell him that what would really be cool was if he told others about Jesus—the most important thing in life—and his friends went to heaven with him. With that, the young man acknowledged the truth in Cahill's words.

Today, cherish the important things in your life, but don't forget to live out the most important thing—serving Christ!

GO:

1. What are the most important things in your life?

2. Is following Jesus the most important thing to you?

3. Today, how can you start to share your faith with others?

WORKOUT:

Matthew 28:18–20
Mark 12:30
Philippians 3:12–15

One Day Better Commitment

After reading the sports devotional book *One Day Better*, I have decided that I need to make the following changes/commitments to grow as an athlete and family member and in my life with Christ:

_____

_____

_____

_____

_____

_____

_____

_____

_____

Signature

_____

Date